Labor Productivity and Profits

By Quentin R. Skrabec Jr., PhD

ISBN 0-7414-3890-9

Cover: University of Findlay- Sam Carter, SIPE Students.

Published by:

INFIꝎITY
PUBLISHING.COM

1094 New DeHaven Street, Suite 100
West Conshohocken, PA 19428-2713
Info@buybooksontheweb.com
www.buybooksontheweb.com
Toll-free (877) BUY BOOK
Local Phone (610) 941-9999
Fax (610) 941-9959

Printed in the United States of America

Printed on Recycled Paper

Published March 2007

To Lady of Fatima and St. Michael

Introduction

Some of the chapters include a fictional interview of key historical figures to illustrate issues. These are researched and based on actual writings. The interviewer is a fictional character named Thomas Magarac.

Thomas Magarac is a fictional *Pittsburgh Press* reporter and son of the mythical steelworker Joe Magarac. Thomas has won many awards for his articles on the fate of American industry and manufacturing. A graduate of Carnegie-Mellon University in Engineering and the University of Michigan in International Business, Thomas has studied the decline of American industry from both a technical and a social perspective. He has worked for the *Pittsburgh Press* since 1976. His father remains a legend in the nearby Monongahela steel valley, as well as his mother, who was the daughter of railroad hero John Henry. Young Thomas remembers his dad's great steel making exploits, as do many in Western Pennsylvania. Joe had worked two 12-hour shifts a day, one at the Homestead open-hearths and one at the Braddock furnaces of Edgar Thomson Works. During World War II, Joe Magarac helped the Monongahela Valley out produce the whole nation of Germany. Joe represented the greatest industrial might the world had ever known. Joe rose to foreman of his Slovak and Hungarian crew and put his enthusiasm into the steel he produced. He had eaten polena kapusta at the White House. He was part of the Brooklyn Bridge, the Empire State Building, the Golden State Bridge, the Sherman tanks in France, and America's great aircraft carriers. For almost a hundred years Joe Magarac ruled the steel valleys until the great industrial recession of the early 1970s that forewarned of the new movement of globalization. Joe realized that the Industrial Revolution was over, and he wanted his son Thomas to have something better than a mill job. Joe is on medical leave now, somewhat depressed, after seeing his town of Braddock, once an industrial jewel, become a town of vacant lots and burnt out buildings. Joe's blood has been weakened by the lack of national iron and steel production, and the lack of sulfur in the air has made breathing difficult. Thomas, an award-winning writer, remains obsessed with the factors that have changed the industrial prosperity of his youth.

Thomas remembered the old days as a boy in Braddock with his father, especially the boom days of the 1950s. Since 1875, Braddock was and remains the home of Andrew Carnegie's first steel mill. Many even believed that Braddock would become the steel city, not its down river rival- Pittsburgh. In the 1940s and 1950s, Edgar Thomson Works recaptured some of its old glory. The town had three movie theaters and several department stores. Many people preferred to shop in Braddock versus the congestion of Pittsburgh. The Works even affected the weather with mill moisture induced snows on cold January nights and night dark afternoons from the smoke. There were, however, days of fun at nearby Kennywood Park and Pirate baseball in Pittsburgh. Streetcars on the 64 and 67 line rushed people between Braddock and Pittsburgh. Today, the clear skies reveal little of that glory. The term ghost town is often used to describe Braddock. Newspapers point to Braddock as a poster child for globalization.

Thomas Magarac has questioned the premise that American business is a causality of globalization. His father had told him that globalization existed in the 1800s, but the creativity of the bosses, industry leaders and politicians had defeated it. Moreover, the workingman had prepared and adjusted to the threats of such problems in Joe's day. The great industrial bosses had overcome the challenges of cheap labor and predator governments, but how had these bosses created such an economic engine? Tom set out to interview the icons of the past who had been successful in a global environment. Clearly, these icons were able to inspire

2

workers like Joe in the steel industry, Paul Bunyan in lumber, Mike Finn in shipping, and John Henry in the railroad industry. Enthusiasm, motivation, and good business sense had triumphed over cheap labor, government intervention, and economic manipulation. History also records a burst of creativity and invention in Joe's day that was unequaled. Magarac started his search for the secrets of early American industrial successes with some of the great icons of the 19th and 20th century. These old icons then held some secrets that might help. Thomas needed to talk to the bosses of these men, and for that he needed the help of an old friend of his father-Tubalcain, the industrial angel. Tubalcain had been assigned early on the guardianship of American industry and business. Thomas was ready to meet Tubalcain who could line up a series of interviews with greats, such as Samuel Gompers, Charles Schwab, Adam Smith, Frank and Lillian Galbreath, Fredrick Taylor, Adam Smith, Andrew Carnegie, George Westinghouse, and others.

Chapter One

Globalization, Free Trade, and Protectionism

Since the death of feudalism, the world has struggled between socialism and capitalism. It has been, to a large degree, a choice of two extremes. Winston Churchill summarized it best: " The inherent vice of capitalism is the unequal sharing of blessings; the inherent virtue of socialism is the equal sharing of miseries." While both systems are subject to man's failings, it is capitalism that this book is interested in. Capitalism exploits man's basic nature, and therefore, capitalism is at the border of man's weakness. Many have observed the natural tendency of capitalism to enlarge class differences, as well as a propensity to exploit the lowest of the classes. It was these very weaknesses that allowed the growth of socialism and the communist theories of Marx and Lenin in the 19th and 20th century. Capitalism's weaknesses can, however, be a strength as well. The profit motivation drives capitalism to improve society as a whole. Students of operations management need to understand the ancient struggle of socialism and capitalism.

America, however, has branded its own type of capitalism known as the 'American System." While Europe and Russia resolved the problems of capitalism with socialist and communist governments, America incorporated capitalism into its democratic system. In communism, government, business, and economics become one. In socialism, government, business, and economics become interrelated. It is only in American capitalism that government and business remain separate, but in some harmony. It is a definite partnership; however, it is on the balancing point of socialism and capitalism. America had to learn how to strike that balance through many failures, but it never doubted the separation at a philosophical level. Government at first played the role of observer, but with government's inability to cajole fairness, it realized it would need laws to control it. The Progressivism of Teddy Roosevelt brought a new role of an empowered referee. Ultimately, the New Deal of the 1930s brought in a touch of socialism into American capitalism to reduce class differences via the government. Some may even view the American system as a blend of capitalism and socialism (hopefully more capitalism).

America's path to capitalism and democracy was unique to the American experience. It is based in our history and cultural experiences. Our colonial experience was one of manufacturing suppression and over-taxation. England forced an agricultural economy on America. Independence brought a desire for economic independence and manufacturing sufficiency. By the 1830s, America was becoming a manufacturing nation. The Whig party and later the Republican Party took on the platform to protect and grow American industry. The self-sufficient agrarian paradise that Thomas Jefferson envisioned was replaced by manufacturing self-sufficiency. By 1898 America surpassed Britain in steel production, machine tools, coal mining, and oil refining. Manufacturing was the core of America's economic success. On August 22, 1878, the *Times of London* hailed American manufacturing with "the American mechanizes as an old Greek sculpted, as Venetian painted." Few years earlier, the *Atlantic Monthly* proclaimed that engineering was the national genius of America. It is the decline of American manufacturing that today heralds a loss of America core achievement for the world.

On May 6, 2005, I happened to be in Detroit. The Detroit papers, radio, and all media were focused on the morning headline that General Motors and Ford bonds were reduced to junk bond status. This stunning result of Globalization started the search for blame. The day reminded me of another day almost twenty years earlier. When I was in the Monongahela Valley outside Pittsburgh. That morning headlines heralded the first time in over a hundred fifty years that no blast furnace was making iron. This event was just as amazing; after all, the Monongahela Valley had produced more steel than Germany and Japan during World War Two. Between these two days, other cities came to hear the bells of Globalization. The day came that tires were no longer made in Akron, glass in Toledo, and steel in Youngstown. A businessman once said that the search for blame is never unproductive. The answers to this defeat of American manufacturing pride were similar in all these cities. These included the overwhelming demands of the union for wages and health care of the retirees. Management shared the blame with lack of investing in new equipment and short range thinking for profits. Then, of course, there are the uncontrollable, the price of oil and energy shortages. Government needs some of the blame as well with trade policies, environmental standards, etc., Another factor (blame would not be correct) is the loss of a belief in America's industrial manifest destiny.

The real problem is attitude; blame is not the issue. The leveling of American manufacturing cities is a result of globalization, which puts all input needs on a global competition. Globalization follows the basic economic principles of Adam Smith penned over two hundred years ago. Globalization has always existed, but its impact has been exponential, with accelerated effects coming from information, technology and transportation technology. The bottom line is the winner will always be the cheapest and most efficient resource. The economic factors of the early industrial revolution dictated that cheap labor be brought to the factory. Today technology allows the factory to be brought to the source of cheap labor. Traditional areas of blame such as the unions, poor management, and lack of investment actually offer little in helping to solve the problematic effects of globalization. In fact, they only delay the first step in solving it-acceptance. The search for blame can waste the precious time needed to adjust to the exponential pace of globalization. Steel, rubber and many other basic industries spent that critical time doing just that. Finally, America has lost sense of national destiny and replaced it with a world destiny. America no longer claimed world leadership, but aspired to be only another country in a global community.

What can be done? Acceptance comes first, and that requires a hard look at the situation. For the individual it may mean a career change or new skills training. The company may have to decide to change its business or radically modify what it does. For both the company and individual, a new level of cooperation is required. The basic tools of change needed are cooperation, high technology, and a new paradigm. Government, labor, and management must come together politically to address the issue. Maybe just as important we need to question what we want our role to be in globalization.

Globalization is not new; Adam Smith defined its core structure over two hundred years ago. The first wave of globalization actually built early manufacturing in the United States. It is actually what brought Libbey Glass to Toledo and Carnegie Steel to Pittsburgh. Libbey Glass, for example, was able to leverage resource and environmental advantages to take glass manufacture away from England and the North American east coast. What is new is the speed and depth of globalization's impact. Information and distribution technology have linked the world, allowing the principles of Adam Smith to be fast-forwarded. Globalization affects employees, small businesses, corporations, and unions in various ways, but economic principles apply. Cheap labor will dominate unless countered by other economic factors. In the 1800s, America brought cheap labor to our factories; now, we take our factories to the cheap labor. New technology allows the Internet to connect us to cheap service labor without any physical movement. A firm's clerical, engineering, customer service, and accounting functions can be performed thousands of miles from the physical plant. Outsourcing to cheaper, English-speaking labor in India is only good business and that's a hard fact. The experimental use of cheap Internet labor by MacDonald's to run its drive-thru shows the depth of globalization, using a clerk in India to communicate with the kitchen.

The extent and results of Globalization are sobering. It makes the price of American labor uncompetitive in the world market and changes social infrastructure. It forces the use of technology not so much for advantage as for survival. The impact is not only on manufacturing, but a wide range of businesses. Up scale retailers face cheaper mock Chinese products in leather, fur, gold, and other expensive materials. Even dentists and eye care professionals will feel the impact as companies reduce and eliminate benefits. In 1970s I attended a grand opening of a neighbor's optometry office in Pittsburgh. It was very elaborate event; I alone was from the steel industry and somewhat looked down on at this affair. As the drinks flowed, the discussion turned to the recent wage increases of the steelworkers and how they were overpaid. My friend had two German cars, which he was proud to point to their superior quality. In 1982, the steel mill down the hill from his high-class suburban location closed, putting over 10,000 steelworkers out of work. Within two years my friend was in bankruptcy court. The problem was those overpaid steelworkers had full eye insurance coverage. He found out too late that his business was heavily dependent on those overpaid steelworkers! Globalization will change local society and structure; one only need visit the manufacturing cities and towns today. The arm of that change reaches into the best of neighborhoods.

Most of the stakeholders have tried to battle it out in the political arena of unilateral wage and benefit demands. Tariffs, anti-dumping laws, and trade restrictions can offer temporary political aid. Some like the dentists may ignore it until it knocks at their door. While these offer some relief, they are unlikely to regain long run advantage for a business. Still, targeted tariffs will probably be necessary to assure the manufacturing future of the United States. Reducing labor costs and benefits, again can offer some relief for the established industrials, but it's an uphill fight. In the 1990s, most steelmakers came to the economic reality that if the steelworkers worked for free, the cost of steel produced would still be more than the price of Brazilian and Russian steel coming into this country. Of course, some of this difference resulted from dumping, but again short-term dumping is inherent to globalization. The lag time, energy, poor odds of success and expense to stop dumping politically can actually be counter- productive strategy for domestic companies. Political strategies are merely part of an overall strategy, not a solution in itself. One successful, but unpopular strategy to counter steel dumping was for the steel companies to buy semi finished dumped steel and finish processing it. The union still had to deal with the loss of the upstream jobs, and they restricted the company's use of the strategy. Still, the fastest and best counter strategy is to actually use dumped product to your advantage. Dumped product is not sustainable, since it is being sold below cost. But by the time political and legal restraints are applied, the damage is done.

Protectionism is considered a dirty word and its existence is opposition to capitalism. Yet, for almost a hundred years, America strived under a combination of capitalism and protectionism. It started with a powerful speaker of the House, Henry Clay, in the 1830s. Tariffs were imposed to protect and allow developing America industry. Abraham Lincoln took on the ideas of Henry Clay with further tariffs. Then the Republican Party of the 1880s and 1890s further expanded tariffs. The period of 1860 to 1920, is unquestionably, America's period of greatest growth. It was an industrial Mecca. Abuse of protectionism on international level created forces that many believed led to the 1930s depression. Still, the great era of protectionism should be studied by all as another alternative to the present policy of "free" trade.

Many manufacturers will argue that America can be self-sufficient! They are probably wrong, but certainly isolation, tariffs, and taxes can be applied to better advantage to American manufacture. These ideas offer hope to the embattled laborers, small retailers, and middle managers of today. It almost seems like common sense that its own manufacturers could supply the great American market. The problem is neither American political parties have any real interest in such a solution. The last president to sponsor a controlled global market was William McKinley in the late 1890s. He held to a complex system of tariffs requiring reciprocity between trading countries. It required constant supervision by Congress to manage the fairness (which might be energies better focused than today). Congress had to penalize abuses of both home industries and foreign importers. Decisions were based on economics and labor concerns. Many, of course, claim they were short on labor concerns, but to their credit, international politics did not play in the decision (America was self-focused at the time with little forgiven political interests). The result was an unequaled economic expansion.

This expansion would not be at the expense of the home industrial base, but would spring from that very base. While McKinley envisioned a new type of international trade, trade relations would be based on reciprocity, not "free" trade. He would not trade high paying American jobs, which he believed were the right of America's democratic success, for cheap consumer goods. Those jobs had been made for with American blood. It was clearly American industrial expansion without any apologies. He based his model on that of his friend and supporter, George Westinghouse, whose Pittsburgh workshops and workers supplied over ninety countries with railroad brakes and equipment. Such a model required the maintenance of a frail alliance of business and labor. It was a celebration of capitalism that realized that "the problem with capitalism is capitalists." McKinley had used his enormous popularity to hold this capitalistic alliance together in the face of the abuses of the capitalists. Yet it was also a simple philosophy based on the voters of his industrial hometown of Canton, Ohio. Simply put, the best thing for American worker were high paying, long term jobs, and the only way to secure and create jobs was through the expansion of business. It was this "dinner-pail Republicanism" that was at the root of McKinley's popularity, America's industrial growth, and political success of the Republican party. His vision of the great capitalistic alliance of labor and owners monitored by the government sunk with his assassination in 1901. We need a McKinley type of policy. Yes it requires a lot of oversight and study by politicians, but that's why they yet paid the big bucks. Simplistic economic solutions require unrealistic assumptions.

The Assumptions of Free Market Capitalism.

Globalization is the ultimate in free market capitalism, but it requires some assumptions of market behavior. Economists today see global free markets as the cure for the dreaded inflation. All of us, who lived through the inflation of the 1970s, find it strange to see the active restraint of inflation today. Gold, energy, and commodity prices in both periods reflected inflation, but today wages and consumer prices are restrained. It doesn't take a degree in economics to understand why. Cheap, foreign, in particular, Chinese products have flooded the American market. Consumers have benefited by these lower prices. Global competition has not only restrained prices but also increased the quality and reliability of our products. Politicians are elected by consumers, which explains the "free trade" logic of both parties.

Control of inflation always comes at a price (really a type of tax) on heavy industry. Jobs are lost, wages reduced, and benefits are reduced as a result of cheap labor competition. Labor competition also presses wages down and that contains inflation by wage increases, which ran rampant in the 1970s. Many argue (correctly) that much of the international labor competition is unfair. Socialistic governments are willing to subsidize heavy industry because of its high employment. Therefore, we are competing against government subsidies, banking trusts, and national alliances. It explains why Brazilian and Russian steel arrives fully processed at a lower price than the American raw material costs. If the American steelworkers worked for free, their steel would still cost more! Adam Smith would argue it is still better for American consumers to buy cheap Russian and Chinese steel, but even Adam Smith realized economics is not a science free of politics. He conceded to the British politicians of the 1800s that shipbuilding should be considered a core national industry, and core industries should be protected. America seems to be missing the point of the era of protectionism that America is special. It is a blend of freedom, democracy, capitalism, and protectionism, and that is what is lost today.

The most violated assumption is economic. If money exchange rates are subjected to a free market, then one might expect some inequalities in prices and wages to be compensated for. The problem is that the biggest competitors in this global market have employment and manufacturing infrastructure goals, not free market trade goals. China, as other socialist countries, try to hold the exchange low to assure cheap prices for their goods, thus maintaining high employment. A free-floating currency would adjust the differences in prices and wages via the exchange to some degree. There are other money issues as well. Foreign companies don't compete in free capital markets, often getting capital direct from the government. To view the global market as a free market is naive at best; but American leadership is not naïve, it wants to lead countries into a world free market. Recent Democratic and Republican administrations seem to have total agreement over the last 30 years. The objective was to spread democracy through free trade, but the problem is you can't have free trade without democracy. Socialist countries will take advantage of you via free trade to gain full employment. Manufacturing managers need a better understanding of economics and politics to help change this. They need to argue in concise and detailed manner. Management and labor need also to realize the common ground here, and question the politician versus the party approach or party loyalty. Business and labor need to build a McKinley type political alliance.

This brings in another problem. Managers, employees, unions, and small business owners don't understand the economics of globalization. Our government representatives are making key decisions on exchange rates, favored trade, tariffs, and taxes with an illiterate electorate watching them. Conservatives had been where protectionists could be found, but today conservatives are free traders, leaving protectionists homeless. Free trade economists from the Chicago school have dominated administrations since Kennedy. With both conservatives and liberals split, there is no place for protectionism. In fact, many conservatives have come to believe that free trade is the very foundation of capitalism, and that capitalism cannot exist without free trade. The real fact is that most of early American capitalists were far from free traders. Certainly, it can be argued that free trade and capitalism would go hand in hand in a unified world.

Democracy

In my heart, I will always be a McKinley Republican, but I find little company today, at least, where it counts - in Washington. McKinley delayed the application of Adam Smith's free trade concepts for a hundred years. The arrival

14

of Teddy Roosevelt's progressivism addressing labor abuses and corporate trusts, the first World War that made America an international player, and the 1930s depression, which many blamed on world trade barriers, ended America's era of exceptionalism. As an international trader and player, things changed forever in America. Different strategies for all stakeholders would have to be applied. These strategies require a level of union-management cooperation and government oversight not generally seen in recent years.

At the heart of the McKinley tariffs was the concept of reciprocity. If a country were to become a trading partner then something in return was required. That something had to have economic value. Teddy Roosevelt expanded that to political returns. Today we get neither. It is our hope that free markets will spread democracy. China would appear to be taking such a path as well as Russia. Long run democracy and free trade are related, but democracy should come first. Regardless, our path seems to be one of global free trade. This forces us to fight in a market, which allows government monopolies. Our anti-trust laws need to be looked at because global competition is big capital competition. Alliances, joint ventures, and mergers may well be needed to over come foreign economies of scale. If we are to be free traders, then we need to be allowed to compete with huge government monopolies in China, Russia, and Japan. We need the economy of scale found in Microsoft. The political problem continues to be our inconsistencies. We are modern free traders that believe in protectionist antitrust law.

The biggest problem all stakeholders have is acceptance of the economic reality of globalization and the American government's will to pursue it. We want to fight it, with government, but trade restrictions are only short term at best, and neither political party shows much interest in tariffs. Force a firm to use higher price labor or resources through tariffs and ultimately, the firm becomes uncompetitive. As an ex-steelmaker, I hate to admit the only real solution is to become globally competitive. This means today, the employee, business, union, government, and corporation must develop global advantage cooperatively. Of course, the fear (and reality) is that American labor is not price competitive. Our standard of living demands not only higher wages, but also costly benefits such as health care and environmental protection. Our companies compete against global companies as well as labor burdened by none of these. The answer is not to require our companies and labor to compete with these disadvantages. We must learn to develop strategic strengths that can offset cheaper global labor and products. Core strengths need protection, even Adam Smith would agree. The deeper government issue is tariffs and "free" trade has not been well managed since the McKinley administration. As an industrialist, businessman, or capitalist, we did to try to move politicians to the old "American system," but strategically, that will never happen.

Globalization, not only puts products in competition, but wages, benefits, cultures, government policies, and social systems. The struggle is huge and runs deep in many dimensions. It's the type of competition that few have seen. Employees will have to trade "givens," such as high wages and generous benefits for risk investment in the companies they work for. New alliances will be needed between business, labor, management, communities, and politicians. This fierce competition, maybe considered social Darwinism that is survival of the fittest. But we need to remember one of Darwin's most overlooked ideas: "It is not the strongest of species who survive, nor the most intelligent, but the ones most responsive to change." Even more recently, neo-Darwinists in biology believe that species that cooperate the most have high survival rates. The same is true in economic competition. An alliance of a community, political party, labor, and management can be a much more formable force in a fight. Still, workers are the most vulnerable in the competition.

The good news is that global advantage is not based on labor costs alone. With the exception of farming and some service functions (where migrant labor applies), America cannot expect to compete on labor costs. What is left then? Technology is required for a corporation, like an MBA is for an executive. It rarely, however, results in a long-term sustainable advantage, yet it must be pursued aggressively. Technology advantages tend to be short term, but they are a necessary part of being globally competitive. Technology is a process of staying competitive. Technology, however, moves quickly in a global market. Successful companies, such as Apple and Microsoft, build technology into their culture. Globalization, however, allows technology to be disseminated quickly. Free-range globalization among countries can be problematic when intellectual rights are not protected. The biggest problem with China is not so much cheap labor as stealing of patented and copyrighted technology. Technology alone, therefore, cannot sustain global advantage.

Managers need to realize that it is not technology, but innovation that is necessary to gain advantage in global markets, innovation being a broader term than technology or invention. It literally means *new* approaches. In many ways innovation applies to everything, but it is easier to segment factors to manage. Global advantage can be developed by flexibility, innovation, and cooperation. Innovation, however, embodies technology and creativity and can lead to a long-term market edge. Innovation combines smoothly with marketing that can gain market share through new products. Innovation is the often forgotten engine of the first industrial revolution as well as today's information revolution. Libbey Glass faced global competition for from its earliest beginning but offset labor disadvantages with product creativity and innovation. Today, we need innovation in benefits, wage, and pension management. Government, whichever strategy it selects, must coordinate with labor, management, and the consumer.

Flexibility is the touchstone of the global organization or employee. Students and employees need to be building skills and preparing for alternative careers, just as corporations need to look for ancillary profit streams. Investment advisors have preached diversity for decades, and the same logic applies to globalization. It's not just a willingness to change, but developing the ability and skills to make the change. Competitive survival in globalization requires a long-term strategy and preparation.

Finally, cooperative advantage is the mark of success, not competitive advantage in a global market. Cooperation even with your competitors is necessary. Sharing resources and people, is all part of cooperative advantage. Two electric utilities sharing overload maintenance crews reduce costs for both. Two gas stations in a small town sharing a tow-truck is another example. It maybe small retailers sharing warehousing or distribution networks. It requires cooperation on many levels, such as government, community, union, management, and nations. While social Darwinism has preached "survival of the fittest," Darwin's own words say it best, "It is not the strongest of the species who survive, nor the most intelligent, but the ones most responsive to change."

What Can the Individual Do?

Acceptance of the global movement must be the first step. You can vote and support politicians that will protect our industries, but never count on it as a strategy in itself. Assume the worse case of free market in a hopelessly unfair marketplace. The individual like the corporation must be competitive, and that means tough head on competition, not outside governmental controls. The answer is in skills, planning, training, and education. The individual must be ready to change careers with the global marketplace. The key characteristic is flexibility and diversification in all phases of your career. Job specialization should be considered only as a short-term tactic. Consider these global, foundational steps.

1. Start to develop an alternative career plan immediately

If you're an accountant, for example, start a part time teaching career or a part time tax business. In almost any career field you can start to develop a future career consulting in that area. It could also be a small side business started on a part time basis. It maybe a writing career that skills are developed prior to any income being generated. Even the recently hired college graduate, must start the alternative plan immediately. In any case, an alternative career plan is a key step in globalization.

2. Select jobs based on additional factors, such as training, education, and alternative career opportunities

High paying jobs can become a weakness, not strength in global markets. Salary commonly enslaves employees, which ultimately leads to dependence. In a global market it's better to achieve your pay through multiple jobs than a single high paying job. The college student needs to major and minor in diverse fields, not specialization. Diversity and flexibility go hand-in-hand for the global employee.

3. Aggressive savings

There is no substitute for savings; your central strategy for globalization must be maximum savings. Multiple retirement plans are also key.

4. Diversify on the job

Volunteer for cross-functional committees and assignments outside your specialty. Take all the training offered.

5. Learn your customers

This is both corporate and personal strategy. Customers offer a way to diversify your product and industry knowledge and expertise.

6. Implement your alternative careers in steps

Start part-time teaching, build a customer file for future consulting, take a new degree program, plan a future business, or start writing for trade journals to build your alternative career slowly. Set objectives and review them.

7. Switch jobs for stability, advancement, diversification, but rarely for money

Short-term salary gains are the Achilles heel of the global employee. Often the very problematic companies in a global market are the highest paying. Many are caught in high paying jobs in rapidly declining industries. So often I see college graduates go to the highest bidder by a few dollars, with no regard to global factors, such as industry, retirement, investment opportunities, and educational benefits. Short-term thinking is the devil of globalization.

8. Maximize college degrees with diversification

With a little planning a student can double major/double minor with little or no cost or time. Add certificates and licenses when ever possible.

9. Keep up with technology

This may require local courses, seminars, or corporate opportunities. Technology is the best tool of the global employees.

10. Develop a cooperative strategy

The employee like the successful corporation needs to form cooperative alliances. Without cooperation, globalization will overtake you and your organization.

What Can a Business Do?

The approach of businesses centers on the same factors of education, technology, flexibility, and cooperative advantage. Many of these will be covered in more detail later.

1. Promote Education

But tie reimbursement to longevity or to requiring a number of years at the company. College graduates change jobs three times at least in the first five years. That makes immediate tuition payback an investment loss. Use focused internal courses and training opportunities.

2. Promote technology

Make technology available in the workplace, but just as important is to use hobbies and contests whenever possible. Tie pay levels to technology skills.

3. Focus on employment versus benefits

In a capitalist free market, employment is a benefit. Companies cannot be social service centers. Bill Gates started early on to set aside cash account so he could pay his employees through the worst of times. Today that account is over 16 billion dollars! The Japanese have guaranteed employment in many areas. Many American companies use a six-month guarantee, which is statistically the time needed in the worst of recessions. The non-working time can be used for training.

4. Encourage self savings and shared insurance

Health benefits and retirement put companies at a unique disadvantage in a global market. Many have forgotten that such corporate benefits were limited prior to the Great Depression. Still, there are many cooperative plans for health care and retirement. Making the employee part of the problem in this case will help resolve the problem. Co pays have been shown to bring down health expenses. 401k's and offer a mutual approach to retirement. Offer financial advising and training.

5. Offer opportunity for upward movement

Opportunity is what most people want as much as money. Promote from within unless major change is called for.

6. Bring politicians in to discuss issues important to the company and employee

With globalization labor and capital must form alliances.

7. Train employees on the economics of globalization

We need to build common alliances among management, union, community, and employees on the issues. These common alliances can then lead to political alliances.

An Interview with Adam Smith

Adam Smith (1723-1790) was considered the father of liberal capitalism. He was a Scottish social scientist. He believed in as little of government interference as possible. He believed in natural performing markets free of politics. At the time, his economic views were a radical break from classical economics. He based his theories on the basic instincts of man in a free environment. His classic, the Wealth of Nations, *was published in 1776, and it remains one of the most read books in history. Wealth of Nations envisioned the globalized markets of today. Smith remained a free trader all of his life. Ultimately, the British adopted his views on trade in the 19th century. His view of free trade, supply side economics, and low taxes has been embraced in the last fifty years.*

Magarac: It's a real honor to meet someone who has changed the thinking of the modern world. In this respect, your only competitor is Darwin.

Smith: Actually, I believe Darwin took my ideas on competition! Survival of the fittest fits my theory better than Darwin's.

Magarac: Only yesterday, the *Wall Street Journal* referred to you in support of outsourcing as well as buying the cheapest product available. What are your views on protectionism?

Smith: "To give the monopoly of the home market to produce of domestic industry, in any particular art or manufacture, is in some measure to direct private people in what manner they ought to employ their capitals, and must, in almost all cases, be either a useless or a hurtful regulation. If the produce of domestic can be brought there as cheap as that of foreign industry, the regulation is evidently useless. If it cannot it must be hurtful."[1]

Magarac: In what way is it hurtful?

Smith: "It is a maxim of every prudent master of a family, never to attempt to make at home what will cost him more to make than to buy. The tailor does not attempt to make his own shoes, but buys them from a shoemaker. The shoemaker does not attempt to make his own clothes, but employs a tailor. What is prudence in the conduct of every private family can scarce be folly in that of a great kingdom. If a foreign country can supply us with a commodity cheaper them we ourselves can make it, better buy it of them with

---

[1] Adam Smith, *Wealth of Nations,* [originally published in 1776], (Prometheus Books: New York, 1991), p 352

some part of the produce of our own industry, employed in a way in which we have some advantage."[2]

Magarac: President McKinley warned me of your debating skills. Your theory is based on the consumer only, not the bigger picture. Take your example to the simplest extreme. If a country is made up of a tailor and shoemaker, and the tailor buys all his shoes from another village and the shoemaker buys all his clothes from another village, wouldn't both be unemployed, and ultimately, the village will cease to exist?

Smith: "If the free importation of foreign manufacturers were permitted, several of the home manufactures would probably suffer, and some of them, perhaps, go to ruin altogether, and a considerable part of the stock and industry at present employed in them, would be forced to find out some other employment." This is the nature of competition. Supporting inefficiency is bad economic and business strategy.

Magarac: Still, this assumes everybody is playing by the same political, economic, and social rules. How about competing against industries that are supported by government to assure full employment in their countries?

Smith: You're not a bad debater yourself. I must admit most of my arguments were based on the British tariffs on agricultural products versus manufacturing. To that degree I was more focused on city dwellers, which needed cheaper food, and my theory of manufactures was also based on the "wretched monopolies" of the time. In Britain, our tariffs on manufactured products produced monopolies that raised prices on the consumer. Tariff free imports kept the manufacturers honest and competitive. At least McKinley tried to control monopolistic pricing. Certainly, I wrote prior to the ideas of socialism and communism, although we had

---

[2] Same, p 353- these are direct quotes

24

very nationalistic monarchies. I guess in fairness, I assumed capitalism as the underlying economic system.

Magarac: So you used free trade to 'govern' the abuse and bad behavior of your capitalists?

Smith: I prefer economic free market as a better control than government action. Even your McKinley, the apostle of protectionism, could not control the growth of trusts and monopolies under protective tariffs. In my experience, the price increases of monopolies are oppressive and resulted in a poor class of urban dwellers. Tariffs become the fortresses of the politically powerful. Look at your present tariff on badly needed ethanol for your farmers while the country is starved for ethanol. Monopolies and trusts also tend to strive with protectionism.

Protectionism unifies domestic producers, and 'people of the same trade seldom meet together for even merriment and diversion, but the conversation ends in some conspiracy against the public, or in some contrivance to raise prices." Free trade produces intense competition, which is the best anti-trust policy for a nation. If it wasn't for this basic human tendency to conspire, I would be supportive of trusts because of their efficiency of production.

Magarac: You have a very negative view of human nature. Isn't that the underlying value of your system?

Smith: It's a realistic view. Nations need the self-correcting effect of free markets. If a nation decides to increase market share by selling under the cost of production, it will erode its wealth. The wealth of a nation depends on production efficiency.

Magarac: Still, doesn't free trade reduce the wages and erode national wealth?

Smith: You have read my book!

Magarac: Yes and while you argue for free trade, you also argue for high wages in the domestic manufacturing industry?

Smith: I suppose in your time, this is a bit of paradox. I strongly believe that high wages are part of national wealth too. "The liberal reward of labor is it encourages the propagation, so it increases the industry of the common people. The wages of labor are the encouragement of industry, which, like every other human quality improves in proportion to the encouragement it receives." [3] your recent interview with Henry Ford confirmed my belief. His breakthrough wage of $5 an hour increased the economy and the sales of the cars he was manufacturing. I argued that wages should be motivational based on production, not necessarily by the hour, although that was the typical method. Higher paid workers perform better, but there must be a relationship between performance and wages. This is where the disconnect comes in. Wages should be tied to the profits of the manufacturers. Wages should go up as profits do, and possibly down when profits go down. I saw manufacturers' profits rise with tariff protection, prices rose, and wages reduced.

Magarac: In today's global labor market, free trade drives wages down, not up. My hometown of Braddock, once a great steel center, is today a rust filled ghetto.

Smith: The issue is the inflexibility and the restriction of labor. Labor must also be freely traded. For example, you have too much unskilled labor in your present mix. I argued that this is the role of government to direct labor to the areas of high employment through training and skills development. If a nation, city, or town becomes dependent on any one type of industry, it will, by economic law, know booms and busts. Diversity is a requirement in the free trade model. Education and training are necessary, not optional. In my day, the

---

[3] Smith, p 86

British government even controlled apprenticeships to prevent surplus labor in any area. Economically, the loss of unskilled jobs to cheaper labor will in the long run increase the skills and education of your workforce. Large employers of unskilled labor, such as your steel mills in the 1950s, created a social dependence. By the 1970s, your steelworkers were managing much more than their college educated managers. There was an imbalance that would be naturally adjusted in the economy. I realize that in the transition, these are trying times for all, but hopefully it illustrates the need for diversity in skills and education.

A worker must diversify and improve skills throughout his career. Companies rarely strategically allow themselves to become too dependent on any one product, service, or customer without suffering the boom and bust cycle. Assuming they are financially strong enough to weather the bust part of the cycle, labor or towns can suffer from the same fate. We need to direct our youth and our youth have to be open to diversity. This is what is lacking in your application of my free market principles. If labor will not or cannot diversify, then it will demand socialism to protect jobs.

Magarac: I certainly agree with the diversification of skills, but you started your book with the benefits of division of labor. How does that fit?

Smith: I realized the limitations of labor division later in my life. I was more interested in the methodology of efficient production versus its economic impact. You are right; division of labor is the basis of assembly line manufacture that favors manufacturers at the expense of the laborer. It is a powerful methodology for operating the management of unskilled labor, but for the last two hundred years we have been moving away from the need for unskilled labor. Assembly line workers are losers in a globalized economy because the lowest price unskilled laborer will always win in such an environment.

Magarac: It's hard to argue your model if you assume your premises. You basically assume men will act unethically in the capitalistic economic model, but will act rationally and ethically on the political level?

Smith: Actually, I ignore the political factors to a large degree. I see the economic factors as overriding. I reason on a basic level on how a village would behave, and extend the logic to international trade. It doesn't matter whether a chief or anarchy rules the village.

Magarac: You make some good points, but you protected your own shipping and transportation industry in Britain during your times. It was law that all imports came in on British ships, isn't this a bit hypocritical?

Smith: Yes, I see your point. I defended this practice on the fact there were two exceptions to free trade. One was national defense and the other was to defend against aggressive trade relations. You have studied the *Wealth of Nations* in detail and found my weaknesses! Shipping and its maritime industry were the heart and soul of England. I supported the Navigation Act that made British shipping a monopoly. When all was lost, it was British sea power that remained. While I never said or wrote it, my actions supported a core national industry in the case of shipping. Actually, a side benefit of our merchant marine industry was that we benefited from free trade. Certainly, it was a bit hypocritical and even nationalistic. It opens me up to criticism. I see where you might argue the same for your steel and automotive industry.

Magarac: Well, let's move to what you think American industry should do in this global market?

Smith: Today's markets are as close to my idealized views that I have seen in two hundred years, and so many of my principles apply. In addition, your advanced technology and communications speed the interactions I defined. I think you, as a nation must decide what is core to you economically. For an outsider, your behavior would suggest farming, but I doubt many Americans would agree. This is where you have the strongest tariffs, government supports, and emphasis. Amazingly, even the solution appears to be directed to farming and the production of alcohol-ethanol. Manufacturing and even your high tech industries appear to have been assessed as non-core, but still important. I think some of this is reflective of your different political directions. You lack national strategic goals in many areas; this lack of strategy weakens you. Without national strategic economic goals, you will continue to falter. Personally, I would suggest high tech be made your core national competency, since it is central to defense as well, and given that your tax dollars should be spent to support and foster it. You are spending far too much on international politics while your economic base is being eroded. To be an international power, you must remain an economic power. They are, as in my day, interrelated.

I would recommend that you reduce taxes related to business and industry except where money is needed for the common good of business and industry. If you want free trade and manufacturing prosperity, you need to reduce taxes on business. Education and skills development need even more emphasis through out your system. Education is fundamental, yet you have let this decline in your country. While I have suggested you make high tech your national focus, you lack the educational basis for the future. I mean, education, in the broadest sense. You need scholarships, better-trained teachers, motivational programs for the sciences, and competition. Government money should always be spent on the common good. Goals, education, and lower taxes are basic to my economic theory. On the negative side, the more painful approach might be to reduce your standard of living, but Americans have never wanted to accept this. Britain has accepted this approach over the centuries, but I doubt Americans can.

Magarac: I don't believe that Americans are willing nor should they be made to reduce standard of living. Why should we subsidize socialism, monarchies, and communism through a reduction in our standard of living?

Smith: Of course, that is difficult to gain agreement on, but free trade promotes capitalism. China's success in trade has occurred along side a movement towards capitalism in that country. Socialism leads to protectionism, so I would argue that your reduction in standard of living is financing the growth of capitalism. I argued in *The Wealth of Nations* that unfair trade problems needed to be addressed economically, but you spend your time trying to politically arrange the world using your market as the tool. This is where you vary from my ideas of free trade. I believe that eventually you will lose your market power as well. I don't believe free trade is causing your economic problems; it is because you are spending economic capital to buy political capital.

Magarac: What can be done with the cartels such as OPEC that we have to deal with?

Smith: Greed will ultimately break cartels and international monopolies long run. The economic laws force replacement and substitution when prices are pushed up quickly and artificially. The worst thing that could happen is a reduction in the price of oil. At the present price, ethanol is profitable. The tar sand reserves, which have the world's biggest oil reserves, are profitable. Hybrid cars are coming into play. The sleeping American government is even starting to awaken. The price rise is the blessing you needed to achieve independence. Not only will you gain independence, but also will create major new domestic businesses.

In my day, wood was the fuel of industry and the consumer. Few remember that by the end of the 18th century we had lumbered out most of the hardwood in England. Like oil today, wood was a strategic resource needed for our core ship building industry. British laws started in the late 1700s to restrict the use of hardwood, so there was plenty of material for the British navy and marine. The real problem was that hardwood produced the charcoal needed to make iron and steel, the driving force of the industrial revolution. There were hundreds of charcoal iron furnaces in England by 1800, and each could consume 6,000 cords of wood or 240 acres of forest a year. The price of hardwood showed similar price increases to oil today in the decades from 1770 to 1820. Local shortages caused economic and fuel supply problems. The price increases and shortage inspired better technology of the furnaces and they became more efficient. A number of inventors arose and made fortunes during this period. In addition, the use of coal in these furnaces was being slowly developed but hardwood remained cheaper into the 1830s. Finally, the price and shortages forced a breakthrough development in the use of coal in the 1840s. With the breakthrough of coal as a fuel, new industries, such as steel making and coal mining, grew the economy. By 1850, coal had completely replaced hardwood in all industrial applications. The cheap and abundant hardwood in the United States until the 1860s caused the United States to actually fall behind in steelmaking and iron making. Economic motivation is the most powerful innovator in the world. More importantly, capitalism adds to the economic motivation, thus capitalistic countries are favored.

Magarac: I have to press the point that markets are not fair and balanced for free trade. We are competing with Asian sweatshops; you can't have free trade in such a world.

Smith: In my day many countries depended on the use of slavery to manufacture. Slavery is not only morally wrong but also economically inefficient. Slaves work at a very reduced rate, and they are not free to maintain their needs. Slaves are not economically free; there is a cost of feeding and providing basic needs. You cannot get high productivity out of slaves or any type of restricted employees. Even in my day, many manufacturing plantations moved from the gang slave system to the task system. The task system allowed the slave to complete a defined task. Then, they could grow their own food, build housing, and hunt. In the task system, the slave owned things and could build wealth. It was still slavery, but it was far more productive. I believe that capitalism can conquer even slave systems in the long run. People perform at high levels when they are free to build wealth.

Chapter Two

"For Whom the Bells Toll"

Free Trade versus Protectionism and the American System

Adam Smith and Free Trade

Adam Smith did not discover capitalism; in fact, the name came after his death. What Adam Smith laid out was the ideal of mercantilism and free trade. He gave powerful arguments for this in his 1776 *Wealth of Nations.* Based on simplistic social examples, Smith demonstrated the efficiency of free markets. Based on assumptions of a democratic infrastructure, decisions based on the common good, and market based labor, Smith built his theory. It is a theory that is hard to refute based on ideal systems. Being Scotch, he was able to win over a following in the British based mercantile system. He made political concessions by excluding British shipping and shipbuilding. Adam Smith justified the exclusion based on its need for defense. He further argued that a country may have inherent core industries, such as the American colonies' agriculture and France's wine making. The same exclusion could be argued today for American manufacturing.

The power of Smith's arguments even made sense to the early United States. Jefferson embraced them envisioning an agricultural society, and believing no need for manufacturing. The powers of Europe at the start of the eighteenth century were basically merchants and traders. Their manufacturing was not threatened at the time by America. Germany and the Prussian states were manufacturers more than merchants and therefore did not except Smith's ideas readily. As America grew and Jefferson found political resistance from Alexander Hamilton's Federalists, free trade versus protectionism of manufacturing became a national debate. It was a debate that would help lead to the Civil War, but would emerge from the war unresolved. Manufacturers heralded the necessity of protectionism for decades, finally losing to the economic reformers after the Great depression of the 1930s.

American System

Even before the Continental Congress issued the Declaration of Independence, it passed a resolution for economic independence. John Adams urged in March 1776, "a society for the improvement of agriculture, arts, manufactures, and commerce, and to maintain a correspondence between such societies, that the rich and numerous natural advantages of this country, for supporting its inhabitants, may not be neglected."[4] Jefferson's agrarian society seemed to dominate after the revolution, until Henry Clay developed the concept of American industrialism and capitalism called the "American System." It was the recognition that independence was as such economic as political. In the 1820s, Clay became the apostle of protectionism. A growing group of Clay Republicans and Whigs continued to develop the philosophy of independence and national dominance through technology and industry. Another driving force was the movement of the rural centers toward new urban centers and growing cities. Jefferson's vision of agricultural independence no longer presented the direction of the country.

Historian John Kasson chronicled the movement into the 1840s:

---

[4] Worthington Ford, editor, *Journals of the Continental Congress, 1744-1789*, (Washington D. C., 1906)

"Republicanism developed into a dynamic ideology consistent with rapid technological innovation and expansion. The older moral imperatives of eighteenth-century republicanism were modified to suit a new age of industrial capitalism. As technological progress offered new stability for republican institutions, luxury lost its taint. For its part, the ideology of republicanism helped to provide a repetitive climate for technological adaptation and innovation. The promise of laborsaving devices strongly appealed to a nation concerned with establishing economic independence, safeguarding moral purity, and promising industry and thrift among her people. So too did the hope that increased production, improved transportation and communications would centralize a country that continued to fear regional fragmentation. Yet the union of technology and republicanism, while settling some issues, raised others. Particularly pressing was the question at whether the new centers of American production, her manufacturing towns, could avoid the blight and degradation of their English counterparts and achieve a new standard as model republican communities. If not, then Jefferson's worst fears might stand confirmed."[5]

The Republican Convention of 1896 presented to William McKinley, its presidential nominee, a well-deserved award. It was a gavel carved from wood of Henry Clay's Homestead reading, "The Father of Protection." Like John Adams, New Englanders seemed to expound this philosophy of economic and technological freedom of McKinley. Writers like Emerson and Hawthorne found this new McKinley industrialism on a level with Jeffersonian ideals. These roots of technological innovation and economic freedom were at the heart of McKinley's dinner pail industrialism. It was the Jeffersonian ideal applied to industrialism. McKinley protectionism prevailed until the

[5] John Kasson, *Civilizing the Machine: Technology and Republican Values in America, 1776-1900,* (Grossman Publishers: New York, 1976), 50

presidency of Woodrow Wilson. Finally the Great Depression was offered as proof of the problems of protectionism. It became economic truth that protection caused the world depression. The economic expansion of McKinley was considered a triumph of innovation, not economic policy.

The McKinley Tariffs: A Manufacturer's Perspective

As part of the economic debate on the North American Trade Agreement and U.S. free trade agreements, many historical perspective papers have again appeared looking at the McKinley Tariff of the Republican Party.[6] Most of these economic views of the McKinley tariffs, and the tinplate tariffs, in particular, conclude that the tariffs were at best, inefficient and at worse, negative. Economists have concluded that the great American manufacturing boom of the late 20th century was not related to the aggressive tariff policies of the Republicans. Interestingly, economists have focused on the tinplate industry, which resulted in the defeat of Congressman McKinley in 1892. Still, today economists point to the tinplate industry of the 1890s as a failure of protectionism.[7] Tinplate, however, is a bias example. In 1890 tinplate was made from mostly imported rolled high quality iron. The tinplaters coated the rolled iron plate with tin through a rolling or coating process. Most of the tin came from Wales, which drove domestic platers costs higher. Two-thirds of their costs were in rolled iron as a raw material, which came mostly from England; thus a tariff on

---

[6] D. A. Irwin, "Did Late Nineteenth Century U.S. Tariffs Promote Infant Industries? Evidence From The Tinplate Industry," NBER Working Paper No. 6835, 1998
And " Changes in US Tariffs: The Role of Import Prices and Commercial Policies," American Economic Review, 88, (September 1998).
[7] D. A. Irwin, "Great Tariff Debate of 1888," *Journal of Economic History*, March, 1998

imported rolled iron products drove tinplate prices high as well. The Welsh producers had an inherent advance processing the world's major tin deposit at Cornwall. In effect, Wales had an international monopoly on tin and tinplate. In the short run, the McKinley tariffs did increase the price of tinplate, but the high price spurred exploration for tin and increased technology investment in tinplate and canning. The tinplate industry itself, however, became a major employer in the United States and prices dropped as the industry matured. Welsh tinplaters immigrated to the United States to set up shop, further building the domestic American tinplate industry.

Dinner-pail or lunch pail Republicanism has become synonymous with the industrial policy of William McKinley.[8] It peaked with the famous McKinley Tariff Bill of 1890, and after a small reduction during 1894, with the Cleveland administration. It became a policy that carried into the 20th century, but Republican senators had been increasing tariffs since 1882. Dinner pails of the time were products of the tin-plate industry, which made tinware for canning and house wares. The tariffs of 1890 protected the infant tin-plate industry in America, but an ancillary result was a short-term price increase in tin products such as dinner pails. Democrats seized the moment in the election of 1892 by sending out tinplate peddlers to sell over priced tinware in McKinley's Ohio district. When rural consumers asked why the price for such things as a tin cup cost so much, the answer was "the McKinley Tariff." Democratic storeowners also increased prices on imported and import-based products to artificial highs. Again when the customer inquired about the high prices, the answer was the same-"the McKinley Tariff." The Democrats claimed that big business was being favored by the tariffs, but one of the biggest American companies suffered the most. The real opposition to the 'tin plate tariff' was Standard Oil whose five-gallon kerosene cans made it's

---

[8] Dinner was the term used for lunch in this historical period

the world's biggest tin-plate user. The tariffs actually forced makers of tinplate cans to become more efficient. McKinley ran a close race with the industrial base of Canton, Ohio but gerrymandering left him short in the election of 1892, after his congressional success with protectionism. McKinley held strong to the long run success of tariffs, and history bares him out.

The McKinley Tariff Act of 1890 is still pointed to as a triumphant policy of protectionism by manufacturers, but it was not always so. In fact, it cost McKinley the only major election he ever lost - the congressional election of 1892. The Ohio democrats in that election used the very name dinner-pail republicanism against him. Prior to 1890, there were a handful of tinplate manufacturers in the United States, but by 1894 there were 200! The tin-plate industry suffered form high price imported iron and steel because of no domestic production, which allowed importers to charge forever. While at the same time cheap tin- plate and tin-plate products were imported in cheaply, which suppressed the development of a domestic industry. The price dropped dramatically by 1895, as the McKinley tariffs created a very competitive iron industry and technology improved through putting profits back into the business. As the price increased American investors poured into the tinplate and canning industry. McKinley, as a Union Army quartermaster, knew well the shortage of canned food to supply the army. The tariffs not only brought investors into tinplate, but into the biggest use of tinplate -canning. During the Civil War, a tinsmith could make sixty cans a day, by 1880 a two-man machine could produce fifteen hundred in one day. In general, the period from 1880 to 1910 saw one of the greatest growth rates for American industry ever. By 1900 McKinley had turned the public perception around; one of the slogans for McKinley's presidential reelection would be a "full dinner pail."

Many recent reviews such as Irwin's argue that the tinplate industry would have arisen in America in ten years, regardless, of the tariffs. This is based on the fact that two-thirds of the cost of tinplate was in rolled iron and steel, and the large drop in the prices of steel and iron in the 1890s. This argument is circular, however, because the McKinley tariffs resulted in almost exponential growth whereas the American steel surpassed the production of Britain in 1898. The tariffs of the 20th century from a manufacturer's perspective were highly successful and the statistical growth of American industry bears that out. The period from 1896 to 1901 when the full force of the McKinley tariffs were in place, electrical equipment production increased 271 percent, steel production increased 155 percent, railroad rail production increased 156 percent, farm equipment increased 149 percent, and shipbuilding increased 211 percent.[9] Average hourly earnings of American industrial increased by 10 percent.[5] Exports grew dramatically as well during the period, leaving the country with a large surplus. The economic boom led McKinley to a strong presidential reelection in 1900. It also built a usual alliance of laborers and capitalists in that victory.

The struggle to protect American industry can be traced to Henry Clay in the 1830s, but Abraham Lincoln, a fan of Clay, brought them to the Republican Party. McKinley, coming from a manufacturing family, had even as a boy debated Lincoln's protectionism in Ohio, coming from a manufacturing family. McKinley had been part of this legislative effort to increase tariffs from 1877. As a member of the Ways and Means Committee, he was instrumental in the formation of a Tariff Commission, and became a framer of the 1882 Tariff Bill. As Chairman of the Ways and Means committee, he again brought protectionism to the forefront. In 1890, McKinley framed a tariff act, which would bring tariff to their highest level. The Democratic Cleveland

[9] Guetter, Fred, *Statistical Tables Relating to the Economic Growth of the United States,* (Philadelphia: McKinley Publishing Co. 1924)
[5] *Historical Statistics of the United States 1789-1945* (Washington, D.C.: U.S. Department of Commerce, 1949)

administration reduced the tariff with the Wilson-Gorman Act of 1894. As President McKinley took tariffs to new highs in 1897 with the Dingley Act. In 1913 when the Democrats took congress, tariffs came down again. The period of 1865 to 1913 was the greatest period of manufacturing growth that the country has ever seen. The period averaged a 4% per year of growth, and reached 7 percent growth during the McKinley administration.

So how do most economists explain the industrial growth and manufacturing expansion through the period of 1865 to 1913? Certainly innovation and invention are offered up first. The impetus for such innovation was not unrelated to tariffs. The period saw the Bessemer process revolutionize steel, the automatic bottle machine revolutionize glass, oil refining revolutionize oil, electric lighting and the application of AC current changing the power industry, and the transportation industry booming. A manufacturer will argue that these innovations came into being as a result of tariffs. Price increases allowed for good profit margins, which encouraged investment back into the business. Carnegie, Libbey, Owens, and Rockefeller all demonstrated this. High employment pushed domestic consumption as Henry Ford demonstrated. Both manufacturers and economists can agree that the period of 1865 to 1913 was one of America's most inventive periods. Charles Murray argues that science and technology actually peaked during this period and has declined since.[10]

Protectionism took the blame in part for the depression, but it was more competitive nationalism than protectionism that created world economic problems. Free trade disciples have controlled both parties since World War II. Reagan was a free trader, but with the heart of McKinley, putting tariffs on machine tools, cars, and steel. Reagan also

---

[10] Charles Murray, *Human Accomplishment: The Pursuit of Excellence in the Arts and Sciences 800 B.C. to 1950,* (New York: HarperCollins, 2003)

championed a 50 percent tariff to save Harley-Davidson, which responded with a manufacturing miracle of new efficiency. In return Reagan saw a rebirth of the old McKinley working class alliance with his party. Since Reagan, however, free trade economics have ruled Washington regardless of party. The period of 1865 to 1913 stands out statistically for manufacturing growth and demands more economic study. The Warren Scoville economic study of the glass industry from 1880 to 1920 supports the manufacturers' view.

The glass industry advanced in exports, production, employment, and innovation under the McKinley tariffs. Scoville clearly shows that the tariffs protected the glass industry from lower cost foreign competition. The response was a price decline, employment boom, heavy reinvestment of the profits, and automatic glassmaking machinery for the first time in 3000 years. Scoville's study even suggests a possible linkage between tariffs and glass innovation that is the tariffs encouraged more risk taking in research and development. An assured level of profitability allows for investment in innovation.

An Interview with William McKinley

William McKinley (1843-1901) was known as the 'apostle of protectionism.' He had fought in 1880 as Chairman of the Ways and Means Committee for America's greatest tariff since that of Henry Clay of the 1830s. McKinley won the presidency in 1896 and again in 1900, but his second term was cut short by an assassin's bullet. McKinley was the son of an iron furnace manager in Poland, Ohio. Later, he would start his legal and political career in industrial Canton, Ohio. As a republican, he pioneered what would come to be known as "dinner pail republicanism." His popularity has waned over the years with changes in political norms, since both national parties have rejected his strong protectionism stand for the last sixty years. He was the last president to build a strong political alliance between the worker and the business capitalists. McKinley envisioned America as a superpower based not on political or military might, but on economic strength. Tom Magarac met the president at one of Canton's famous steak houses, Lucia's, near the McKinley memorial.

Magarac: Mr. President. It's a true honor to meet you.

McKinley: I met your father several times at the White House, and I had the utmost respect for him. I've heard a lot about Lucia's, but it was built long after my Canton days. The town saddens me; it lacks the noise, smoke, and excitement of years ago. That old Republic Steel mill a block over was known as the "birthplace of alloy steel." It saddens me to see it closed down after a hundred years of operation and innovation. It was also the mill where Henry Ford invented vanadium steel for his Model T. As with your dad, these great mill closings weaken my optimism.

Magarac: Dad said you were the only Republican he had ever voted for. That, of course, is why I wanted to interview you. A Republican with such support of labor and business seems strange today. I also thought that the apostle of protectionism should at least be heard again about globalization.

McKinley: I doubt that I would have much support today for my brand of protectionism. It is unfortunate that labor and capitalists aren't united. Their goals are the same, but it was a delicate balance for me. Capitalists can be their own worst enemy, and are more apt to fall to their own greed. Still, my passion for protectionism made me the candidate for both.

Magarac: Protectionism has been considered an evil since the Great Depression. Mr. President, do you believe it has any role in today's world?

McKinley: That, young man is the right question, but I'm not sure I can answer it. You have created much complexity in your world. Politically, protectionism today is what you call a "non-starter," but there are times where it could be of some value to you. I was simply shamelessly pro-American. My vision was the economic empire of America. I believed America was destined to be an economic super power.

Magarac: Your times did seem to be much simpler.

McKinley: Not so much simpler times as simpler visions. We looked at America as exceptional in the march of history, and blessed by providence. It was the economic extension of Manifest Destiny. Regardless of the times, I maintain that tariff duties should be applied according to this simple principle- duties should be high enough to measure the differences between the wages paid for labor at home and in competing countries and to adequately protect American investments and American enterprises.[11] Tariffs are needed to protect the exceptional position of American labor as the defense of freedom. When we pull our wages down to that of underdeveloped and oppressed nations, we do our country a great disservice. We overlook the sacrifices of our citizens for freedom. My trade policy was known as reciprocity because it required economic balance. I was not interested in giving favorable trade relations for alliances, political friendships, and political support. We'd buy your sugar, but I expected you to buy equivalent amount of our goods. My vice-president, Teddy Roosevelt, was from the progressive wing of the party and saw things differently. His vision was an international power, which is yours today. I'm not sure the American worker cares about America as an international political power. American workers want financial freedom and the goods money can buy. I feel I was elected to give them just that.

---

[11] McKinley's 1889 acceptance speech for the Republican nomination.

Magarac: Most of the icons I have interviewed profess a belief in Adam Smith's free trade and are strongly anti-protectionism. Smith argued that if a family could buy something cheaper than they make it, they should buy it. Smith argues that countries, like families, should buy the value available, doesn't that make sense too?

McKinley: Grover Cleveland used it against me constantly. Smith, of course, had a point. His logic is tough to argue with, but it assumes the family has an income. The Irish immigrant workers were some of my biggest supporters, having suffered the logic of England's free trade policy. Trade between our states is free, but between nations, it is never free. There are competing political systems in the mix. I realize that my opinions would never be taken seriously in your globalized market. The idea of protectionism is blamed for the Great Depression and its return would start a wave of trade wars. The facts of America's protectionism and the McKinley tariff tell a very different story.

Magarac: I wanted to interview you so that the alternative view would be aired, but shouldn't we buy where you can buy the cheapest?[12]

McKinley: I say buy where you can buy the easiest, and that spot on earth is where labor wins it highest awards.[13] American labor is the engine of the economy. Henry Ford found that in his record breaking wages to his workers, which actually spurred a boom in the purchasing of automobiles. Tariffs can even create new industries. Prior to our 1890 tariff laws, most of our pearl clothing buttons were made by prison labor in Austria. After 1890, our buttons were produced by American free labor. Before 1890, we employed 500 men at $12 to $15 a week making buttons. By

[12] This question and McKinley's answer were part of a McKinley speech in Boston, October 14, 1892

[13] Same as above- direct from the speech

1892, we employed 8,000 men at a wage of $18 to $35 a week.[14]

Magarac: Didn't the consumer pay the price for these better wages?

McKinley: Prices appeared to go down, but I must admit we probably did spin that a bit. Prices did go down in some sectors because of money that was invested in more efficient production. Government had to assure that the benefits of the tariffs resulted in capital investment, not end up in the pockets of the bankers. Still, I had lived in industrial Ohio all my life, and the ups and downs of the economy were devastating. Employed workers make our nation strong and allow capitalism to foster. Cheap prices mean little to the unemployed worker. Free trade erodes the very heart of your nation. Free trade, if possible, assumes equality in the world. America is exceptional, not equal. I know that this approach is not popular today and even borders on the dangerous edge for many. I'm not saying Americans are better only that they should be rewarded for their sacrifices and efforts to lift up mankind. Capitalism should lead the world for it allows man to achieve his dreams. We need not support systems that actually suppress human creativity, ownership, and innovation. My party fought slavery, which was an example of economic greed and low prices. Look at where your cheaper goods are coming from, and then decide do these laborers have the freedom and protection of American laborers. The tariff and its possible increase in prices for the consumer should be considered a down payment on freedom.

Today you have another incentive to protect home industries. The government relies on and unions demand that big business cover health care and retirement, putting American industry at an enormous disadvantage. You either have to protect these industries or you will have to have government foot the bill. American industry cannot keep

---

[14] Same as above

45

working with such a disadvantage. I would have probably set a tariff to cover the difference in health and benefits. It is frustrating to look at the position of American industry today. We got there for the right reasons, but government, business, and the unions need to be locked in a room to work this out. Once, I sent my political advisor, Mark Hanna, to tell the mine operators that they were "damn fools," not giving the workers their demands and allowing a strike. I made it clear, I have protected them and I expected them to live up to their part of the bargain. Government needs to apply pressure to avoid restrictive legislation.

Magarac: Many viewed you as owned by "Big Business"?

McKinley: That's fair. I supported American business, where else could employment come from? I know at times they abused my support, and that was unfortunate for all. It was a tough balancing act and from what I see remains so today, but that's why people elected you president. I used a quiet approach to keep business in line versus Teddy who followed with a more flamboyant approach. You also have to remember that the bankers were the fourth estate in my day. Even the President of the United States had to pay homage to J. P. Morgan, who functioned as the government's banker prior to the Federal Reserve. Teddy, the great trustbuster, was forced to cut a deal with Morgan on his Steel Trust to bring the nation out of the 1907 Panic.

Magarac: I guess we are not willing as a nation to make that commitment today?

McKinley: That's another variation of man's propensity for greed.

Magarac: Well at least it's not on the level of the Robber barons and bankers like J. P. Morgan!

McKinley: I wouldn't be so sure, young man. Greed is the problem whether the system is socialism or capitalism. Greed is a problem whether it is with the consumers, capitalists, communists, unions, or the bankers. Government's role is to protect us from ourselves. I brought these groups together, so that all could be prosperous in America. When we had full employment, few complained about prices. When jobs were in short supply, it seemed like everything was a problem. My assassin was a product of the recession of 1893, when many turned to socialism and anarchy. Capitalism works best in a full economy, socialism waits for bad times. The numbers of pro-protectionism America are impressive. From 1865 to 1900, U.S. trade actually quintupled from $261 million to $1.53 billion. American industries dominated world value and quality in metals, machinery, metalworking, mining, and transportation. The trade surplus was a staggering $616 million dollars in 1898.

Magarac: Didn't capitalists benefit more than the worker?

McKinley: Capitalists abused the system! Often I had to stand with the unions against abuses in wages after having protected them. This is what government should do - enforce the moral laws against greed. I had the support of the Knights of Labor because they trusted that I would balance these abuses. The basic guiding principle is that the union and management really want the same things. Ideally, they should never be pitted against each other as in socialist countries. One of my problems was the fourth estate of the bankers. Before the formation of the Federal Reserve, the president and manufacturers were beholden to bankers such as J. P. Morgan. Bankers represented a tax on both manufacturers and workers. It was unproductive money, but these bankers did teach us something. J. P. Morgan showed us the importance of economy of scale in increasing profits. Morgan, however, carried things too far with his interlocking directorships and trusts. I wish now I would have been more aggressive with these bank-controlled trusts. The abuses of the trusts would eventually break up the alliance of the workers and manufacturers. Unfortunately, the growth of unions became necessary. Unions such as the United Mine Workers were needed to stop the abuse. As a young lawyer, I defended thirty-three miners imprisoned in Massillon, Ohio in an 1876 strike, and that success launched my political career. I never forgot my early labor roots. On the Ways and Means Committee, I fought tirelessly for railroad safety, when the owners refused to spend the money. It was my dealings on railroad safety that brought me in contact with George Westinghouse. He gave me faith again that the American manufacturer could be fair and profitable, but there are few men like Westinghouse. Government must always be the field referee that is its role in capitalistic systems. Capitalism is a powerful incentive, but it also can challenge the ethical character to the breaking point.

Magarac: In your last speech at the Pan-American Exposition at Buffalo, you suggested the impact of globalization might mean a modifying of your protectionism views. Given the free trade environment today, do you have any small steps that might be taken?

McKinley: My friend and supporter George Westinghouse taught me that America needed to export to expand. Westinghouse was manufacturing American made railroad brakes for sixty countries out of his Pittsburgh plant. Westinghouse Air Brake became our first truly big international company with plants in Europe, Asia, and South America. One downside of my extreme protectionism was a lack of an American merchant marine, which I proposed to rebuild in my Buffalo speech. I realized change was coming, but I centered my new approach on reciprocity-economic reciprocity. I argued that day that the function of government was to assure a positive trade balance and fair-trading. That probably is where I differ most with your "free trade" approach of today.

Therefore, I would look at the countries where the trade balance is most out of line. I was always a great admirer of Japan, and I think the present Japan/United States economic policy is the ideal. Japan has and is building new manufacturing plants in the U.S. This is an example of my principle of reciprocity that I never dreamed of. Reciprocity must be applied in the global market. My major argument with your trade policies today is in the mixing of politics. The trade status with the United States is not based on economic reciprocity, but your politics. The selling off of American jobs for political favors is wrong. Free trade should be based on the fairness of the economics, not your politics. This common practice of economic boycotts is where I agree with Adam Smith that this practice should end except where used to avoid an immediate war. Of course, I support restricting trade with countries that violate human rights, but economic factors must be applied in most cases. Maybe just as important is that trade decisions must reflect the will of the people, not philosophical positions. Another step I strongly believe is the enforcement with any trading partner of intellectual property rights. Political tradeoffs should never be accepted unless it is the full will of the American worker and taxpayer. The American government's only right for existence is serving the will of Americans. I always pandered to my industrial base in Canton and that's why they elected me. I believe trading partners should be encouraged to buy some of our product in return for trade. Lastly, some industries must be protected against unfair trade or even protected to assure American employment. I would never change on my view that the American dinner pail must be filled first!

Magarac: What about the argument that tariffs increase prices?

McKinley: Yes, my experience is that prices will increase slightly, but it's less of a problem when you're working. And yes, some manufacturers will raise prices and retain the profits. Government is charged with the task to monitor such abuses. The market is, to some degree, self policing. Price increases then trigger economic alternatives. Consider your present situation with oil. Your have experienced a quick 50% run up in price. Now you have ethanol technology, tar sands, bio diesel technology, and shale oil kicking in. Capitalist countries are driven by price. Edison, Westinghouse, Ford, and so many others picked their projects based on economic need. We protected the American glass industry and steel industry and got an explosion of technology. Government has the role of making the economics favorable for the American people. I opposed our role as an international power because it got in the way of being an economic power. Take care of the economics and you get everything else. I'm sure most of your readers will at least consider my views a bit extreme by today's standards.

Magarac: I want this study to look at all sides. Maybe, I should get off trade and ask what else might be done to return American manufacturing to dominance?

McKinley: Yes, there were other factors in our great industrial expansion. One was a national pride in industry, manufacturing, and scientific accomplishments. It started with Prince Albert in England and the Great Exposition of 1851 and continued with Napoleon III in France. These expositions and world fairs were the technical Olympics of the times. They grew champions, like Bell, Krupp, Edison, Morse, Westinghouse, Tesla, Bessemer, Colt, and so many others. Competition always favors capitalism. Every exposition, great or small, helped us step forward. Friendly rivalry followed, which spurred further industrial improvement, inspired useful invention, and produced high endeavor in all areas of human activity. Furthermore, these expositions encouraged the study of wants, comforts, and even the whims of the people. The result was improved quality of our products and lower prices. Without such competition we would have clung to clumsy and antiquated processes of farming and manufacturing and the methods of business of long ago and the twentieth century would have been no further advanced than the eighteenth.[15] You saw a similar fostering of innovation in the 1980s with computer fairs. I believe the American government has to get more involved in fostering innovation.

The labor-management alliance needs to be rebuilt. What is good for labor is good for business. Without this alliance, you lack the political power needed. I believe the lack of a national policy on manufacturing today is because of the split of labor and management into their respective parties. Labor and business have more in common. I would hope that one of the major parties would take up the cause, but you need to build the old "dinner-pail" alliance. More likely, however, a grass roots movement of labor-management is needed to support candidates regardless of party. Labor and management today would still remain a formidable political block as did need in my day. Look at China today; its strength is cheap, abundant labor. China lacks innovation and invention, and that is its Achilles heel. Eventually, Chinese labor will demand more pay and their only advantage will shrink.

America can use immigration to participate in this low cost market, but you can see the resistance of this approach. America needs to compete in the higher tech and skilled labor markets. Here again, we see a lack of national direction. Training has been reactive with funds coming from Congress for displaced workers. At the same time, the math and science skills of the nation are approaching those of undeveloped countries. Youths lack the inspiration of technical fairs and competition. It's bigger than math and science, today's students lack problem-solving skills. The labor-management political alliance of my day assured education focused on the needs of business. Industry also invested in technical education. Industry seems to continue to invest in education,

---

[15] McKinley's September 4, 1901 speech at the Buffalo Pan-American Exposition

but it lacks government help. I'm proud to point to a joint program of Ford Motor and my home state of Ohio to develop student skills in problem solving and decision-making. These are missing skills so badly needed in industry and manufacturing today. In my day we needed drafting and shop skills, which motivated men like Charles Schwab and George Westinghouse to build technical high schools.

Magarac: One last question. It has been said you thought being a major in the army was more enjoyable than your years as President.

McKinley: Being president was a true honor, but being a supply officer was in many ways more challenging and satisfying. The real challenge is in those middle management positions, and so is the strength of any organization. Even the President of the United States depends on those middle positions to be successful. The officers of the Civil War were some of the best leaders the world has seen. Great generals always have great officers under them. I truly believe part of today's problems can be traced to demoralized middle management.

Summary

1. Free trade should be a cooperative goal of nations based on economic reciprocity.

2. Reciprocity should be the basis of all trade agreements.

3. Free Trade requires free societies and governments.

4. Socialist countries will abuse free trade to gain jobs.

5. Protectionism should be used for defense industries and designated core industries.

6. Economic policy should be based on the national good, not economic philosophy.

Chapter Three

A Global Approach to Productivity

Measuring Productivity

Productivity is implied in the biblical mandate to "multiply and prosper." The ability to transform natural resources into product remains the distinguishing attribute of mankind over lower life forms. Anthropologists use tool-making ability to classify the evolutionary steps of man. The problem is that productivity is not as simple as many definitions suggest. At its simplest roots, productivity assured the tribe or group's survival. Boosts in productivity beyond subsistence levels, resulted in improvements in quality of life and population growth. The arts and religion could prosper in highly productive tribes because less time was required for basic needs. They probably intuitively understood the relationship between productivity and quality of life, but they lacked the means to measure it. The inability to measure it was a limiting factor of pre historical productivity.

Earliest written history suggests the Sumerians started to measure output some 5000 years ago. They had a system of managerial accounting that allowed for measurement. Once you are capable of measuring productivity, you can make incremental steps to improve it. Most of the Sumerian productivity advances were related to agricultural work, but about the same time, the Egyptians were measuring the productivity of construction work. The Egyptian managerial structure required daily and monthly reporting of progress, and with measurement came the science of improving productivity. With the Egyptians, we see the use of both personnel management and scientific management applied in an effort to improve productivity.

The first writings on labor productivity (output per labor time applied) can be found in the Qin Dynasty of China around the third century. In crafts production records of the Qin Dynasty, labor-days are used as units of comparison.[16] Using labor-days, the Qin Dynasty made comparisons of productivity based on sex, the nature of work, age, and time period. They compared the work of men, women, and juveniles doing various types of work. They even differentiated the labor requirements of different types of iron products. They also used the labor-day statistic to set production goals. Maybe just as revolutionary was the broad understanding of the role of cost and quality in measuring productivity. Manufacturing requirements were specified for quality levels and cost levels. These early Chinese understood that productivity was not a quest for high output, but a quest for efficient high quality output. A rigid and structured inspection system maintained quality under the penalty of death! Like the Egyptians, quality levels were established and only production meeting that level was counted as output. This simple, yet fundamental principle is one that seems to have been lost in the last half of the twentieth century.

The Statistical Process Control and the Deming movement of the 1980s lost sight of the basics of human manufacture and created an inherent disharmony. Independent auditing and inspection are a necessary requirement in the world. The 1980s quality movement suggested that the worker could be his own inspector. Ideally, there is nothing wrong with the concept. The concept evolved from the role of the craftsman to perform both functions. The craftsman, however, exists in a world of limited competition. He was more artist than manufacturer.

---

[16] J. M. Juran, *A History of Managing for Quality,* (Milwaukee: ASQC Quality Press, 1995), 25

Quality was paramount with productivity being a constraint (the reverse of manufacturing environments). It is possible to have an inspector/operator, just is it is possible to have an accountant/auditor for the company books, but human nature is faulted, requiring independent review. In fairness, Deming really only wanted dependence on inspection eliminated, not the inspection function. Robots offer a potential to combine functions in one entity, while maintaining independence of the functions. Cost efficient inspection is however, possible even today, and we will look at it in later chapters.

Even the craftsman/inspector of old is really a myth. We have already seen that the Qin Dynasty had government inspectors for the crafts. The medieval trades were governed, regulated, and inspected to assure quality. The Hebrews reinforced quality through religious laws and proverbs, which often dealt with the accuracy of scales and measures. The biblical references are testimony to the entropic nature of humans in manufacturing systems. In the 1800s in Germany, the government responding to abuses moved to regulate the trades. This included government inspection and product certification. In some cases such as the Purity Laws of the German brewing industry, the raw material quality was regulated. At markets and fairs, similar trades were required to be together, so that competition and comparison could help assure quality. Craftsman marks had to be registered with the government and maintained through government inspection. Yet many continue to point to the era of unregulated quality crafts production. The fact is that production by humans, always leads to compromises and tradeoffs in time, quality, and cost. Quality must be set or constrained by a "governing body," such as the government, corporation, trade group, customers, or as a top management response to competition.

The consumer of any product rarely buys based on quality or cost alone, but on value. Value being defined as quality divided by price. A carpenter may pay a quality premium for a saw, while a homeowner, may opt for a lower price and the corresponding lower quality. Even the craftsman often adjusted his production based on the end customer. The quest for super quality can violate a basic rule- if the customer wants higher quality, they should be willing to pay for it. Some of the highest quality auto industry suppliers went bankrupt trying to improve quality without any payback. The increase in quality often came with a penalty of reduced productivity and increased cost. Part of the problem was another myth of the 1980s that "quality is free." Quality is never free; it requires effort.

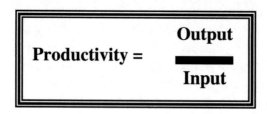

$$\text{Productivity} = \frac{\text{Output}}{\text{Input}}$$

Globalization is, to some degree, self-regulating, that is, like the German grouping of trade markets, it pushes similar product quality up based on competition. Improving quality can be used as a competitive advantage in the market place. Because of this, productivity can never be viewed without the consideration of a required quality level. Quality levels thus complicate the concept and benchmarking of productivity. The productivity of a plant manufacturing screwdrivers for professional mechanics cannot be compared to a plant making screwdrivers for dollar stores. The Qin Dynasty realized this difference over thousand years ago, imposing national quality standards and enforcing them. Productivity is constrained not only by quality but also by cost. Cost must also be looked at as a constraint on productivity. Cost and productivity have a complex relationship that we will deal with in upcoming chapters.

Value = Quality/Cost

Productivity, because of constraints, becomes difficult to benchmark, and to some degree, difficult to fairly measure. Productivity goals can also have inherent pitfalls. Achieving single focused metric productivity goals can lead to quality, service, customer satisfaction, and cost problems. Managers have struggled with the problem since the 1970s. Like the Qin Dynasty, national standards have been one way of setting the level of constraints such as quality and cost. ISO and TS 9000 are examples of such efforts. The problem is that these process or system standards often lack the teeth to assure product consistency. The 1980s saw the popularity of system audits and process control. Many managers are now seeing that diagnostic inspection is the best process control. Testing the product remains the ultimate test of any system or process.

The one approach to measuring and setting metric goals is that of the balanced scorecard. Productivity is not considered as an isolated metric, but one interrelated with many corporate outputs. Productivity, internal quality, customer delivered quality, cost, and delivery, for example, form a package of balanced measures. Process productivity should be monitored and adjusted based on the aggregate of these measures. For those with scientific training, we want to define productivity as a dependent variable (output/input), and then analyze the independent variables that affect it. The Qin Dynasty had an understanding of this basic scientific research approach. This, of course, was at the heart of early practitioners of scientific management such as Taylor, Gilbreth, and Gantt. Quality level therefore is an independent variable that affects productivity. This of course complicates the management of productivity, but puts the focus on good output versus mere output. The balanced scorecard offers concurrent feedback lacking in some productivity measures of good output per input. Good output measures are not timely because of inventories and customer feedback. Quality problems may surface weeks, months, or even years after the physical production.

Dealing with Quality and Productivity

Ideally a productivity measure should capture quality as a dimension but rarely do. The balanced scorecard is the popular approach, but it is far from optimal. Traditional management in America requires productivity and quality be measured separately. Mentally, this creates a struggle between production and quality, and historically, industry looks first to the production measure. The craftsman of an earlier age did not have this mental struggle. Of course, there are good reasons such as the lag time between production and the customer's ultimate acceptance. Therefore, we pay bonuses on product produced in a short time frame such as a shift or day. In the steel industry of the 1990s, I tried but failed to negotiate a piece rate bonus adjusted for returned steel. It was what was needed, but none wanted it from management to the union. Without such an integrated measure, the internal struggle between production and quality is entropic, destroying overall productivity and product quality. It assures mediocre quality and productivity.

Productivity is like Capitalism – It's Self-serving

Productivity is the result of motivated employees, not leadership alone. Productivity and capitalism are interrelated. Communism has failed to match the inherent productivity of capitalistic countries. Even communal arrangements have failed to match self-serving capitalism. The Pilgrims initially had a communal arrangement to share the fruit of their labors. These were good, hard working Christians, but they also had inherent human shortcomings. The land was owned by all and the harvest shared. Governor William Bradford can be considered the first American operations manager. As the arrangement failed, they moved to individual ownership allowing community trading of individual surplus. The result was an amazing turn around in productivity and output. Bradford's journal should be must reading for operations students; it is an experimental log of operating systems and productivity. Freedom and private ownership is critical to productivity.

Slavery was immoral, criminal, and highly inefficient. On a purely economic level it was also a failure. American southern plantation owners, started to realize this too late. Many of the more enlightened owners moved to what was known as the "task system." The task system set out specific daily tasks for the plantation slaves. When the tasks were completed, the slaves were free to farm their own plot, hunt for food, and have leisure time. Slave families built their own homes and had a large degree of freedom. They had rifles to hunt with. They fed themselves and were highly productive in the fields. They received some basic materials and supplies for their communal work, but were basically self-sufficient. Compare this to plantation slaves that worked all day, only to receive poor food and housing supplied by the plantation owner. These examples go to the heart of the nature of productivity. Free people with the hope of personal gain are the most productive. It is at the heart of the failure of communist societies as well. It also explains why socialism in Europe has resulted in reduced productivity. Cooperation is important, but motivation is ultimately an individual effort.

In my own experience when raises are given on an equal basis, mediocrity rules. Merit raises result in high productivity. It is the problem with unions, where pay is based on seniority and raises are equal. Unions can serve an important role in preventing abuse, but they promote low productivity because of the lack of merit. In education no grade systems also produce mediocrity. Competition and gain are part of productivity. Andrew Carnegie's highly productive organizations of the 1800s were rooted in manager ownership (unfortunately, he didn't offer the same to the laborers). There must be the potential of personal gain in capitalism and productivity.

Productivity and Efficiency

For today's manager productivity and efficiency are interchangeable, reflecting output per input. Efficiency is the older term preferred by engineers. Early scientific managers often used the term efficiency. Production, as noted, seemed to have had historical priority. Frank Gilbreth, one of the first efficiency experts, however, noted that the real issue is efficiency, not the amount of production. Engineers lead the scientific management movement and used analogous terms to machine efficiency. Machine efficiency was straightforward as a measure of output divided by input. The first half of the Industrial Revolution was driven by the improvement of machine efficiency. The following looks at the exponential growth of machine efficiency of a 200-year period.

Year	Engine Type	Percentage Efficiency
1718	Newcomen	.5
1767	Smeaton	1.4
1792	Watt	4.5
1816	Compound	7.5
1834	Cornish Engine	17.0
1878	Corliss	19.0
1906	Triple Expansion	23.0
1918	Steam Turbine	65.0

The engineer simply measures the coal BTU input to the BTUs of engine output.

Machine efficiency could be standardized to some degree because an engine does the same thing over and over again. Quality and cost could be assumed to be standardized. These Victorian engineers soon found that the human productivity cannot be equated with machine efficiency, and struggled with the correct measurement. Humans behave too inconsistently to use measures of engineering efficiency. Efficiency seemed to be a simple measure for many years.

In a society where slave labor was available, overseers often measured only output. Ancient Egypt was one example of slave labor production. By the late 1800s, in most western societies, slave labor had economic penalties and efficiency became important as we have seen. Slave overseers moved from the pure slave system to a task system, particularly in manufacturing environments. The task system allowed the slave to complete a set of tasks followed by personal time for hunting, cooking, and caring of family needs. The task system proved more efficient overall to the overseers. Less time was needed for the tasks and costs such as feeding etc., were reduced. As slave labor disappeared, labor cost became a key factor in efficiency and productivity. As resources become scarce, efficiency becomes more important. Labor productivity (output per labor hour) has been measured by the U.S. government since 1888.

Productivity of humans is a complex and a multifactor attribute. Labor productivity could be measured, but its management was another issue. Engine efficiency is based on the consistent work of an engine; human work is not consistent. Engineers first wanted to standardize work and human motion, so that machine efficiency principles could apply. This resulted in the scientific management movement of Fredrick Taylor. Scientific management was indeed an improvement, but its goal of robotic operation was not achievable. Certainly, we can expect robots of the future to approach machine efficiency, but human behavior is not consistent. Fatigue, learning level, best practices, quality expectations, and process knowledge are a few of many factors that come to play on productivity. These complications need to be managed, but the measurements of productivity should remain simple like those of the Qin Dynasty, who used the basic statistics for more complex analysis of the variables that affect productivity. More complex measures can be used as an analysis tool, but not for goals.

There is always a tendency to scale or factor our measures of productivity. We start to mix management and measurement, and in doing so we harm the role of metric goals to motivate. Take the case of Lion Department Store in Toledo, Ohio, which for years measured sales productivity of its employees as sales dollars per hour. When Dillard's purchased the Lion store, they wanted to tie pay more directly to productivity. This would require some adjustments, such as the department you worked in (high price items versus low price), the day you worked (weekend versus weekday), the time of day, sales promotions, etc. The new adjusted number was reported weekly to the employee, but the complexity of the calculation left the employee clueless of their day to day impact. This type of indexing of pay can defeat the very goal of productivity improvement. From the employee's standpoint, metric reporting needs to be simple and straightforward. Analysis is the role of the manager.

The Productivity Paradox

Increases in efficiency and productivity have a surprising result; it increases employment, payroll, and production. Unions for decades, like the Luddites of the early 19th century, feared automation and productivity improvements because such improvements would eliminate jobs. The fact is the very opposite is always true. One of the best examples is that of the 19th century glass industry. The glass industry was one of the world's earliest and largest employers. For almost 2000 years, the labor-intensive methods of glass manufacture remained unchanged. Over a ten-year period at the beginning of the twentieth century, Mike Owens automated the bottle making process. The result was not a drop in employment but a major boom. The reason was the dramatic increase in bottle making productivity, reduced prices. Initially, there was a slight drop in employment, but it was followed by a major upturn. The reason was lower prices opened up massive new markets, such as milk bottles, beer bottles, and soda pop bottles. This is typical of history. The efficiency of Ford's assembly line reduced the price of automobiles to the budget of the average American causing a consumer boom.

This appears to be a paradox, but with a little history, it becomes the first law of productivity; that is, productivity increases lead to increased employment. The PC revolution created a major industry instead of the job reductions that many foresaw. Even the Luddites of 1812 were ultimately amazed to see that power looms resulted in a world wide boom in cloth and textile production. James Watt's steam power created massive industries such as the railroads, mining, and construction that many times increased employment beyond the initial reduction. Cheaper resources result in more use and new markets. The union should always embrace increases in productivity, but fear seems to rule. Steel unions in the 1980s opposed their employee's participation in productivity improvements. Productivity initiatives were even prohibited from employee improvement team discussions. The fear was further job cuts, but the fact was lower productivity cost more jobs. Furthermore, a result of the first law of productivity is that an increase in productivity ultimately increases wages. While there are a few exceptions, the most productive companies are the highest paying. Another result is that productivity assures future jobs, not the opposite.

Still the old adage - that it's a recession if your neighbor loses his job and a depression if you lose your job, applies. Automation and productivity improvements can lead to a brief and initial job reduction. If we look at the early 1900s bottle making revolution, we see a cooperative plan that held wages and employment steady during the first years of automation. Mike Owens created a true revolution in glass bottle making in 1914. A six skilled man glassblowing crew could produce 15 gross pint beer bottles in 8 hours; one of Owens machines with one operator would produce 500 gross pint beer bottles in 8 hours. Prices went from $3.75 a gross to $2.50 a gross.[17]To Mike Owens credit he worked short term to ease the pain of job loss. Glassblowers were converted to high paying machine operators, and conversion was paced with employee training. It wasn't perfect but it was a peaceful and somewhat painless conversion. Within two years, the price of bottles dropped dramatically and the market for glass bottles mushroomed. Glass industry employment tripled. Employees and employers need to be full partners in the expansion of productivity.

The real paradox of automation is its long-term impact on employment. Automation can lead to exponential employment growth by reducing costs and increasing markets as we have seen in the cotton, steel, and glass industries. In the 1860s, the Bessemer steel process took steel from an expensive material of craftsman to the dominant constructional material in the world. In twenty years, the Bessemer steel plant of Carnegie in Braddock, Pennsylvania, employed more steelworkers than the world had employed twenty years earlier. Of course, in the short run fear of lost labor can slow automation. Carnegie and brilliant plant manager, Bill Jones, were relentless in applying new technology as soon as it became available. Known as the "scrap heap policy" even brand new equipment was replaced if better technology became

---

[17] *National Glass Budget,* October 21, 1911

available under Carnegie and Jones. Their decisions were not determined nor dependent on accounting payback methods. Reduction of product cost was their implementation rule. Even MacDonald's found that the implementation of automated tellers quickly resulted in a 25% in business and a 10% in employment. I like to call this the Carnegie-Jones-Owens law of automation. Long run automation results in lower costs, lower prices, market growth, and increased employment. It should be hung in every union hall.

Problems in the Measurement of Output

Human productivity becomes even more multifaceted when you move to intellectual, service, and office work. Now the problem becomes how to measure the output; for example, how do you measure the output of an administrative office, a college, research center, or service department? One problem in the late 20th century was the use of qualitative measures of output for intellectual, service, and office work, but the competitive nature of the global world demands. Thomas Edison created an 'invention factory" at his Menlo Park compound in the 1890s, by using metric goals. His stated goal was a "major invention every six weeks and a minor one every six days" This focused his organization on a measurable output metric. The productivity of Edison at three thousand plus inventions remains unmatched even today.

Another approach used by project managers is event driven. This approach goes back to scientific managers such as Henry Gantt, who used it for factory and machine loading. Event driven approach is really a series of time goals laid out on a Gantt or project chart. Traditionally office management used time goals as well as project management techiques. A manager would specify a report due in three weeks or better on August 15. Project can use events such as digging of the foundation.

Improving Productivity

Productivity can be improved by improved machine efficiency, human motivation, and improving the machine/human relationship. Machine efficiency is improved through technology. Engineers might well argue that productivity is machine or automation driven, but the human factor is far from obsolete. Until we have fully autonomous robots, humans will be the real detriment of productivity, not the human alone but the human/machine interaction. Inherent motivational issues at the worker/work interface capped Ford's assembly line's productivity. Often high tech software results in a decline in productivity because of poor worker/work interface. Applied technology at the user level must be simple and friendly.

The worker must be motivated and that it requires the worker to see some type of gain in his effort. That gain could be financial or achievement oriented, but it must exist. In the end analysis, productivity is very personal. Each worker makes a decision on the level of effort he or she applies. That decision is made daily. Rewards must be timely to support that daily decision. Like Provo's dogs, we like treats immediately if possible. Furthermore, productivity is competitive at its root. Productivity lends itself to numerical tracking and goal setting. Shift and plant competition alone can contribute to productivity gains. Some managers have been brilliant in exploiting this basic principle and relationship of competition and productivity. It also explains some of the poor productivity of socialistic countries.

The Role of Government

Government has a vested interest in productivity, since it defines the nation's standard of living. The problem is that government has become the third estate instead of an extension of both labor and capital. Government needs to assure the education and motivation of the workforce. On the other hand, government has shifted responsibility for health care and pensions on corporations while asking them to compete with unburdened world corporations. At least most agree in an educated labor force, but this will not make American corporations competitive alone as we have seen. The great innovations of the 1860 to 1920 period were not from education but economic motivation. The government needs to rigorously protect intellectual and patent rights, making it a component of trade agreements. Manufacturers need to demand this from China. Manufacturers need to form associations to develop more political power and to voice the problems louder.

The government cannot set economic trade policies without taking the responsibility to assure its fairness. Government for its part needs to motivate innovation through educational programs, contests, and national goals. We need to emphasize science, math, and engineering more. Our youth needs to become more competitive not less. We need technical Olympics like the old World Fairs. Government scholarships and grants should re-build our science and engineering. The problem is many Americans see American firms as responsible for the downfall, when government has been the problem. You can't put pensions and health on corporations and expect them to be competitive. Pensions and heath care account for an additional $2000 to $4000 per car. If we are to be free traders, then government must take those expenses on instead of burdening the product's ability to compete in a global market. The problem has reached the point where we need a national policy on manufacturing.

Finally, government needs to reduce taxes to increase personal gain. The link between personal gain and productivity is extremely strong. There is of course always the danger of abuse and again government has a role to play. Still, abusive companies, as seen in our slavery example, are highly inefficient, and really perform under their potential.

The government has to assure balance without freedom and capitalism. Free men in capitalistic societies are highly productive. Government must play the role of facilitator in any case. Private ownership is also a key factor in productivity and should be promoted by the government. Government should promote individual savings and financial responsibility.

An Interview with Samuel Gompers

Samuel Gompers (1850-1924) is considered by many as the father of the American labor movement. Born in London, he became a naturalized citizen in 1863. In 1864, he joined the Cigar Makers' International Union. By 1885, he rose to president of the Cigar Makers' Local 144. He led the Cigar Makers' into the Federation of Organized Trades and Labor Councils. In 1886, he founded the American Federation of Labor, which grew in four years to represent 250,000 workers. The American Federation of Labor was the forerunner of the AFL-CIO and the United Automakers. His goal was to achieve rights for the worker without political affiliation, using strikes and boycotts. He viewed the union as the labor component of business on equal footing with management. In 1920, he formed the first International Labor Organization under the League of Nations. Later in life he worked to spread unionism throughout South America. Magarac met Gompers at the Homestead, Pennsylvania, 1892 Strike Memorial near the Waterfront Mall that now sits where the great Homestead steel plant stood.

Magarac: I'm glad you could meet me at the Homestead 1892 Strike Memorial. My father taught me that this spot is sacred for all laborers.

Gompers: It's sacred for all of American industry. Homestead is symbolic of what must not happen in labor disputes, we "need to recognize that peaceful industry is necessary to successful civilized life."[18] The strike typifies classical management/union failure, in that; we see lack of communication, hard headed stands, huge egos, uncontrolled tempers, and the inability to listen. Neither Carnegie nor I were here, but I think we both regret the deaths and mistakes. Both Carnegie and I tried to learn from the failures so prevalent here. The memorial offers a reminder and a hope for all. If I had my way every manager and every union member would have to visit here and read the story of the Homestead Strike.

Magarac: Many have criticized you as being too conservative or too soft. How do you see your legacy?

Gompers: Slow progress is best; this memorial is a testimony to moving too fast. Henry Frick wanted fast results and that broke any hope to settle. I wanted slow progress in all negotiations, not revolutionary progress. "One might have imagined by what is often considered as the solution of the labor problem that a world cataclysm would take place to resolve it." Karl Marx and the socialists of my day certainly believed this. "They believed they would go to bed one night under one system and wake with a revolution in full blast, and the next day they would organize a heaven on earth. That is not the way that progress is made; that is not the way the social evolution is brought about. You need to solve the problem day by day. As you win an hour's more leisure everyday it means millions of golden hours of opportunities to the human family. As you get 25 cents more a day wages increase, it means another solution, another problem solved." I focused the union on local issues, plant by plant, avoiding philosophy. Unlike the socialist wing of my union, I believed progress should be made locally. Laborers are first interested

---

[18] Testimony of Samuel Gompers, *Report of the Industrial Commission, 1897,* (Section VII, 604)

in their own workplace, not the nation's philosophical labor policy.[19]

Magarac: How do you feel about the one party union policy of today?

Gompers: As president of the union, I had a non-political policy, but it was difficult to maintain. In the 1870s, the Knights of Labor formed its own party known as the National Labor Union. The National Labor Union managed to nominate a presidential candidate in 1872, but not much else. Personally, I strongly supported the Republican McKinley tariff of 1890 but tried not to publicly join the Republicans. Most of us were Republicans because of those strong tariffs. I realized you needed work before wage increases. Still, we kept the Democrats somewhat honest by not signing a formal agreement with the Republicans. The Cleveland Democratic tariff reductions, the Homestead Strike, and the Depression of 1893 created a new challenge. The Socialist Labor Party signed many of our members. The socialists, while a minority, were able to split the labor movement. McKinley's victory of 1896 was a labor victory because of the return of tariffs.

I remain strongly committed to a non-political party alliance. Labor today is tied too closely to one party, and that allows the other freedom not to be responsive to labor. Politicians would be supported, not by party affiliation, but by their record. The political policy of the unions today is unfortunate. The crisis today requires both parties to be part of the solution. The issues of trade, immigration, and cheap foreign labor are too broad for any one party. Politics is not the union's strength; I learned this the hard way. You need to bring the politicians to conferences regardless of party. I started an active lobbying effort that addressed both parties. Even with McKinley, we tried to stay non-political. We let

---

[19] Edward Kirkland, *Industry comes of Age,* (New York: Holt, Rinehart and Winston, 1961) 362

our members know that McKinley would be best and let them deliver the votes. We did not finance his campaign. The one party system of today's union is a huge mistake. It can become a political millstone for your "buy American" campaigns. The Southern Republicans consistently support "buy-American," but become frustrated with the contention of the autoworkers with the Democrats. On the other hand, you need to develop some pro-labor Republicans in the Southern states to support labor legislation. While many point to my support of Republican McKinley, they often forget my support of Central Union Labor candidate over Republican Teddy Roosevelt and the Democrats. Principles before party must be the rule.

Magarac: Many in your own labor movement criticized your relationship with business and the Republicans.

Gompers: I stood for jobs and steady wage increases as profits increased. Daily wages and earnings increased 50 percent from 1860 to 1890, and real wages increased 60 percent during the period.[20] You can't get wage increases when profits are coming down. Furthermore, I worked with new technology and automation instead of opposing it on principle. There is a positive and strong correlation between profits, wages, and employment. The union should always be pro-business. I was a capitalist, and you need cooperation in capitalistic society. Government's role should be limited to regulating abuses, not market conditions.

Magarac: Many claimed you were too pro business with your dislike of antitrust legislation. Do you regret that approach?

Gompers: "When Senator Sherman proposed to forbid by law the development of industrial combinations, I felt that

---

[20] Ross Robertson, *History of the American History,* (New York: Harcourt, 1973), 379

his theory was fundamentally wrong. The greater efficiency that follows unification of control and management benefits society through increased production. Sustained progress of industry prohibition, and non-social tendencies can best be curbed by intelligence."[21] Here I agreed with J. P. Morgan that you gain efficiency with size, and you are seeing this with your international competitors. In many cases you are competing with huge, national corporations. On regulation, I agreed with the McKinley Republicans, who applied pressure based on common sense.

Magarac: You believe in non-partisan political action don't you?

Gompers: Action on direct labor issues but not philosophical issues. Our union split with the internal socialists was over a union sponsored program to nationalize telegraphs, telephones, railroads, public utilities, and mines in the 1890s. These were obviously the pet ideas of the socialists. I fought hard to keep the union focused on union issues. The decline of the first great labor union, the Knights of Labor however, declined rapidly from 1888 on due to some anarchists in the organization. The Knights became political activists. We did support boycotts against firms backing non-union practices. It's difficult because you are part of problem and need the political system. If I were in charge of the union today, I would be lobbying both parties for tariff relief for major industries. We need to look at what defines "free trade." We need to form an alliance again between capital and labor for America, and I feel the union will have to forge that alliance. An alliance between labor and capital represents the strongest political block possible. Today we have labor and capital in political opposition, and I believe American labor loses in that environment. To me, political action by unions was a socialist and Marxist vision I wanted to avoid. Today

---

[21] Samuel Gompers, *Seventy Years of Life and Labor,* (Gompers: 1925)

political action is needed to define a national labor policy. You have no policy today. Furthermore, the political parties should be called upon to support and ratify union programs, not the other way around.

Magarac: While you avoided political action, you did become active in immigration legislation?

Gompers: In 1910, I said the immigration problem was really a "labor problem." The situation is the same today as it has been since the 1860s. "America must not be overwhelmed. Every effort to enact immigration legislation must expect to meet a number of hostile forces and, in particular, two hostile forces of considerable strength, requiring a counter force. One of these is composed of corporation employers who desire to employ physical strength at the lowest possible wage and who prefer a rapidly revolving labor supply at low wages to a regular supply of American wage earners at fair wages. The other is composed of racial groups in the United States who oppose all restrictive legislation because they want the doors left open to an influx of their countrymen regardless of the menace to the people of their adopted country."[22] American labor loses when immigration is unchecked. These are things government should be involved with.

Magarac: Would you support a boycott of Wal-Mart?

Gompers: Certainly that is a tough question. I think a peaceful consumer boycott is appropriate, but I think the issue is bigger than Wal-Mart's policy. It goes to the heart of our lack of a national policy or strategy on globalization. In one-way Wal-Mart is creating badly needed jobs. They are not practicing child abuse or unsafe working conditions. I think their lower pay reflects the problem of globalization. The fact is that our present national policy dictates lower

---

[22] From a letter to Congress by Samuel Gompers dated March 19, 1924.

wages and benefits in the future. We see the very symbol of American industrial might- General Motors- near bankruptcy. The auto suppliers are there already. Today we're not striking against rich robber barons, but cheap Chinese labor, which wins either way. In my day, the union role was to assure that prosperity was shared fairly; today it is to spread the pain fairly. Yes, I would be screaming for the return of the McKinley Tariff instead of striking or boycotting.

Magarac: Do you still believe in not resisting or striking over the implementation of labor reducing methods and machinery?

Gompers: Yes, and I learned the futility of resisting progress, especially in a global market. I called a strike once against the introduction of cigar molds and methods that would have reduced some job reduction. We held the company back, only to lose many times more jobs to foreign competitors who implemented them and employed very cheap labor. In particular, Bohemian cigar makers who had a government monopoly and hired cheap female labor. I learned that resistance was futile. In the 1890s, we worked with Michael Owens in automated glass bottle making, and created huge new markets and jobs for the glass industry. The global market is dominated by government monopolies, which will adopt technology and take market share. In today's market, amazingly, it would be prudent for the union to be in the forefront of applying technology.

Magarac: Is there a major role for the union in today's global market?

Gompers: I must admit that, looking at the impact of globalization of our great industries, the future looks unmanageable. Steel, forging, casting, metalworking, and even the automotive industries have been humbled. In many cases, we are looking at wage preservation versus increases.

This is a national crisis of industry. If ever an alliance of capital and labor is needed it is today. We need innovative approaches to the problem; our experiences are of little use. Labor and capital truly need to re-invent the workplace for this new environment. The union issue today is not so much with management as with our national industrial policy or lack of one. China is behaving as we did in the last quarter of the 19th century with the same success we saw.

Magarac: You always favored highly skilled labor over unskilled. Do you feel the corporations, unions, and the country need to move toward more skilled labor replacement of unskilled labor?

Gompers: I believed that shift would have occurred years ago, but I was wrong. Unskilled labor remained decade after decade. To a large degree the union prolonged its existence. In any case it has arrived in America. Chinese have the massive labor base to apply unskilled labor to their advantage. Without tariffs American unskilled labor is not competitive; in fact, even with tariffs it would be difficult. America's strength and future is in skilled labor. Actually, labor is not the right term. In my day, we talked of the craftsman, but for today, technician is more descriptive. The education and skills set is probably equal to two years of college. Computer literacy certainly will be a requirement. This new skilled labor is right for America, and it's an area we should excel in. Robots will eventually replace the unskilled labor even in developing countries. My fear is that whole industries are moving out of America, and there will be no base to build on.

We fought hard to retain our glass, steel, and machine industry through the 1950s, but today we have let those industries go off shore. Our strategy must be to hold on to the big industries in some form. Thanks to our working relationships with the Japanese, the auto manufacturing industry remains with the new Honda and Toyota factories in

America. These transplants pay a good wage that is lower than the traditional big three. They have reasonable benefits, but again estimates suggest the benefit cost is a thousand dollars or more per vehicle less than the Big Three. They are beating the American Autoworker plants significantly on vehicle costs. Yet, we cannot oppose their increase in American jobs. This structural decline in wages cannot be avoided. They have found the industry's and the union's weak spot and are exploiting it. It's a difficult position for both the American unions and industry leadership. It is a direct result of globalization.

Magarac: Sounds like the end of the unions?

Gompers: Not really. The union will always have a role when abuses arise. The abuses today tend to be in the treatment of clerical, office, lower managers, and technicians. Here we see age discrimination and job losses more related to management. Understand that I don't believe in the spreading of unionism for its sake only. George Westinghouse showed that fair treatment is a valid substitute for unions. The real need for unions is probably in Asia and Africa. Internationalism will have to be part of the future of unionism, although I'm not sure what that movement will look like. Labor and labor working conditions need to become part of our trade agreements. Making the playing field level is a future role of the union. The Union and its mission are changing, and I believe when fully morphed, the union will be a much different organization. It will represent the workingman in new and different ways. My guess would be an organization more like a trade association or industry group than a plant organization.

The worker today needs representation in Congress. The issue is no longer the right to organize, strike, or to have better working conditions, but the right to have a job. A McKinley and his dinner pail politics are needed. The union should also focus on spreading unionism in undeveloped countries. I spent my later days spreading unionism in South America to help level the playing field, but the world is too big for American unions to solve the problem. The government needs to act as the referee on the field, penalizing nations when necessary.

Magarac: Should unions fight for pension plans and retiree benefits?

Gompers: Another extremely difficult question. A promise must always be honored in business. Pensioners should be protected and the plans backed by the government. Government polices are responsible for the mess today. Now as far as future pension plans, this will require new approaches. The Great Depression changed management and union. I always believed labor should be paid fairly, and then labor is responsible for its own retirement plans. As an officer for the Cigar Makers' International Union in the 1870s, I helped set up a union managed pension program. I believe the union should manage the pension program with the aid of the company. I viewed the socialism of the 1930s as problematic, in that, pension plans became part of big company benefits. Labor unions probably should offer pension plans to help. You cannot burden product with it as you are learning. Today's 401K's are great tools, and social security must be maintained as the minimum safety net. The free market will not support our social programs, and that is part of the globalization problem. The union should be focused on the economic issues of the worker instead of politics.

Magarac: How do you feel about Adam Smith?

Gompers: Adam Smith makes sense in a perfect world. Smith's insights are basic if you were living in 18th century England. Trade was between civilized nations or their colonies. Slave labor was common throughout the empire. There were no developing nations. America was restricted in most industries except those like tobacco needed for England. His free trade theory was based on trade between European nations. I know you're probably tired of hearing about a level playing field, but that is the issue. Level the field and I'm with Smith.

Magarac: Carnegie, Schwab, and even Henry Ford disagree with protectionism as the answer. They feel the great American expansion of the 20th century was driven by innovation?

Gompers: They probably believed that. They were very positive, self-reliant, proud leaders, but the fact is the tariffs were part of their success. I don't think you can separate out that protection. They also had a cheap labor source of immigrants, and from my perspective, they exploited that labor. In retrospect, we sometimes can come to simplistic solutions. I do credit their innovation and investment polices, but we stood together in the halls of Congress on protectionism. You have to get over the negative association with tariffs. You are exporting jobs and getting little in return.

Magarac: My goal in this project has been to search for agreement and disagreement.

Gompers: Cooperation is the key to successful job creation and improvements in the work place. The walls have to come down before it's too late for both American labor and business. In government, we need a return to dinner pail politics. Fair trade, not free trade. Government must monitor and referee markets, not control markets. Furthermore, I agree with the American exceptionalism of McKinley. The best way to spread democracy is to be economically strong.

Summary

1. Automation will lead to higher productivity, lower prices, and ultimately to higher employment.

2. Automation may reduce jobs short run, but will increase them many fold long run.

3. Goal setting and benchmarking are key tools improve productivity.

4. Productivity is anchored and segmented by quality levels desired.

5. Productivity measured as goals should be simple and straightforward.

6. Robots are the next wave of "cheap" labor

Chapter Four

Inventory – the Barometer of Efficiency and Productivity

Inventory reflects the overall efficiency, quality, and productivity of an organization. It is the most important measure that a company can track, and it can be an effective barometer of corporate health. For example, if you have quality problems, in-process inventory will increase to cover rework and machine bottlenecks. Many astute stock pickers analyze corporate inventory and inventory trends to evaluate investment potential. Companies with poor productivity tend also to build inventory in slow times to handle future bottlenecks. Having been on a design team for a joint American/Japanese venture factory, what became obvious was the Japanese reluctance to have storage space or any excess space. They argued if you give Americans space, they fill it with perpetual inventory. In the current shutdown of glass factories, wonderful pieces of glass products have been found tucked away for years in corners. Several companies actually found old experimental products that have application today. Americans do tend to fill space up just look at the average home.

Measuring inventory and tracking it routinely is avoided by most businesses. The annual inventory count is a rite of passage for any new manager. The waste can be striking to the operations manager as the miscounting is to the accountant. Corporate managers have lost sense of what inventory is. A small business owner knows all too well that his cash is tied up in inventory. Worse inventory is a deprecating asset. University trained managers have no feel for the actual cost of inventory, and may have even been trained to look at it as a customer service. Inventory build can solve many problems such as poorly maintained machines, absenteeism, poor quality, low productivity, delivery problems, poor scheduling, and bad management. Inventory becomes a comfort blanket to many a manager.

Inventory tracking and management should be one of the top priorities of a manager. Benchmarking is key to that process of inventory management. Inventory turnover is measured by the number of inventory turnover per year or days of inventory on hand. Inventory turnover may be seen as structural, and segmental tracking can be helpful for management focus. For example, a department store tends to have two turns per year based on the cold and warm seasons, but some products, such as house wares and jewelry may not have this seasonal impact, and should be monitored separately. We need to segment and track inventory with the same analytical tools we apply to quality tracking.

In the 1990s to meet the demands of the automotive industry for just-in-time delivery most steel and parts suppliers went to perpetual inventories. This resulted in amassing a variety of parts inventory to delivery on demand. The cost was huge sending many into bankruptcy, but there was no other option. Poor quality, in particular, prevented them from supplying on time. The relationship between delivery and quality should be another law of Operations Management

---

Operations Law of Inventory control one

Poor quality is the number reason for late delivery, or it is through the management of quality that you achieve high delivery performance.

Companies that have 3% rework, 3% scrap, and 3% customer returns tend to have a build-in level of 9% in the inventory to meet delivery. That's inventory that is also deprecating and becoming obsolete so it has to be maintained at a huge additional cost. It's a problem many newly graduated managers struggle with. Which comes first implementing Just-In-Time programs or quality programs? College graduates are trained to view them as separate coming from different disciplines, when they are really an integrated problem.

Inventory turnover, dollar trends, and aging need to be tracked monthly, if not weekly. Many wonder today, how did our great manufacturing oriented of the nineteenth and early twentieth century companies produce high quality without quality control departments or programs? Part of the reason was a fanatical management approach to inventory. Poor quality of supplies, in process parts, and final assemblies was the major reason for inventory growth. If you go into factories today, the sheer floor space is tied up in scrap, distressed or held material (for re-inspection), and customer returns are amazing. Distressed or inspection held material is in itself a measure of management efficiency. This material agonizes as it awaits a decision by management. One of the biggest problems remains the need of quality control departments, which started about 1917. That was when we lost our naive understanding of manufacturing. We separated quality and inventory control departmentally, but even worse, we separated them functionally and philosophically. Quality control and inventory control became an internal struggle, and the struggle internalized the trade-offs of production and quality. Even professional societies took sides with the American Society of Quality and the American Society of Production and Inventory Control. A manager should belong to both these societies, or maybe we need an integrated society. Unfortunately, the division is now culturally ingrained in American business.

We talk of making the worker responsible for both production and quality, yet we have separate management departments and functions. It is this management division that restricts the success of making the worker responsible for both quality and production. Workers commonly rejected quality charting of statistically process control programs because the function appeared as a quality control function. The charts went to the quality control office, and management responsibility for chart maintenance was with quality control. The cultural barrier is the problem in obtaining harmony of quality, production, and even safety goals in industry today. It would be better to have a process control department in place of separate quality control and production control.

Harmony is an old term for integration used by Fredrick Taylor. Taylor, the father of scientific management, studied factory integration in 1911. Congress had hired him to study the poor safety record of the steel industry. Congress had really concluded that the push for high production was the cause, and Taylor was hired to confirm this. It seemed what these high production shops would have the poorest safety record. What Taylor found was much different. The safest mills had the best productivity. Taylor argued that if production was pushed over safety then production suffered long run, and the statistics clearly supported it. He also noted a type of harmony in well run steel plants with safety, production, and quality integrated as a management mission.

Computer managed inventory

Bar coding of inventory is a key tool for inventory control. Radio signal chips can even make inventory updates instantaneous and reduce theft. This technology can be a major improvement in inventory monitoring, but what is done with that information is still a problem. Management is needed to "manage" inventory. Knowing the exact status of your inventory doesn't reduce a dollar of inventory. A tough-minded manager can do more than any high tech accounting system, but combine a good manager with high tech system and you have success. Some argue against bar coding's role, preferring the use of Kanban systems, which tend to be more visual and manual. The advantage of Kanban is that it drives understanding. My personal preference is bar coding with good sense. The recent radio signal bar codes offer a level of control never dreamed of a few years ago. Whatever the system-all managers must be trained in its functioning; there can be no substitute for this.

In addition to bar coding, powerful software such as Materials Requirement Planning (MRP) systems are also available. This software takes out managerial error and allows for follow through on strategic goals, but it does not replace good management. This software stills allows for "safety stock," which can build inventory. Managers must still make the strategic and tactical decisions for the software. Care must be taken in managing with software. Complex software can automate things, but managers can lose sense of what's really going on, and that is the heart of the inventory management problem. A balance must be struck on strategic follow through and short-term tactical management of inventory. In any case, if you implement high tech inventory management such as MRP or MRP II, then be sure every manager is trained on the internal functioning of the software. Upper management needs to view the strategic inputs at least every six months, and other managers need to review it weekly. There should be an inventory committee or team established to coordinate and manage levels. Many management philosophers argue whether quality is employee or management owned, but inventory is clearly owned by management.

Module Production

American manufactured products are cogged in an inventory pipeline. Auto inventory can be found at the assembly plants and dealerships. Our sales infrastructure on large manufactured products favors inventory built. Furthermore, as we struggle to offer more product customization, we increase the pressure to build inventory. Inventory built occurs throughout the supply chain with customization. The Henry Ford business model of reduced customization to gain productivity and efficiency does not apply in such a customer environment. In 1920 Michael Owens, the inventor of the automated glass bottle machine, tried to convince bottle users to reduce variety for lower prices of bottles. He failed, learning he would have to adjust his automated machines to handle the market variety. Owens passionate drive achieved that goal in a few years. Almost all markets today demand flexible and variable product manufacture. We have to learn to achieve customization without inventory build.

Module production offers the type of flexibility needed, and we have an American business model available in Dell Computer. Dell combines powerful supply logistics with module design to achieve both goals. Dell uses the advantages of the Internet to eliminate cogged inventory pipelines and retailing middlemen. Furthermore, the Dell model leverages the advantages of globalization, such as cheap sub-assemblies. It uses logistics companies, such as Fed Ex, UPS, and others to achieve speed, inventory reduction, and customer satisfaction. Other manufacturers such as appliance manufacturer Whirlpool is developing similar module manufacturing. Both Ford and GM have been studying the idea for years, but there is resistance in those organizations including the dealerships. Yet, automotive manufacturers could gain even more efficiencies than Dell Computer. It takes about 40,000 pounds of raw material to make a 4000-pound car. Module manufacturing can push the high scrap production to lower labor cost in countries, forcing them to absorb the materials cost.

An Interview with Edward Libbey

Edward Drummond Libbey (1855-1925) put American glass on a par with the great traditions of Europe. Libbey created this American industrial and art revolution through aggressive marketing and high tech processing. He moved his struggling company from New England to allow it to have access to the competitive fuel costs of Toledo, Ohio. While trying to become cost competitive, he launched a world marketing effort. Libbey built a complete glass factory on the midway of the Chicago World's Fair of 1893. His product captured both the American and world market. While he teamed up with Michael Owens for breakthrough technologies, such as bottle making machines and window glass machines, he returned to the lost practices of Europe in producing art glass. He made the glass industry one of the first to be world competitive. Tom met him at his Toledo Art Museum.

Magarac: I could spend days here, studying glass and its history. Does it reflect your global view?

Libbey: I was an American in a traditional European industry. Glass and glass art have deep roots in Europe. 16th century Venice was the birthplace of the beautiful art flint glass and crafts practices to produce it. Up until 1850, almost all glass pieces were imported, with the exception of a few utilitarian pieces. Even Americans believed fully that the best glass was from Europe, and they were not wrong. The high end of the world market belonged to European manufacturing. The very low end of the western states was limited because of breakage in transportation. The European market, in addition, had tariffs on American product. Through government support, they could readily ship low price product into this country. These factors forced me to be global in my approach to glass making.

Magarac: Certainly, many businessmen can relate to these conditions. They sound like today. How did you start the process into the global market?

Libbey: It started at my company, but a few years before I arrived. My father and Deming Jarvis really started the struggle. Jarvis started with a dream to compete with English imports in the city of Boston. He lacked most of the raw materials, had only an inferior fuel available, but even if he had the materials, he lacked the artisans. Getting artisans would be a major problem, since the European laws forbade the emigration of glass artisans. Now that is a true barrier to entry!

Jarvis started with research into the industry. Good cut art glass is around 20% lead and requires an ingredient "red lead," which is a semi-processed ore. Jarvis, an importer tried to import red lead, but the cost was prohibitive. Jarvis used his Yankee ingenuity to read all he could on the manufacture of red lead and built experimental furnaces. Still lacking expertise, Jarvis went on to smuggle Thomas Leighton of Scotland into the country. Thomas Leighton, would by the way, go on to be a leading glass innovator. Jarvis imported all the literature of glassmaking he could get out of Europe. Once, he had cracked the red lead problem, he started into glass production, eventually smuggling Irish and German glasscutters in.

In addition, I spent months studying and touring the European glass houses. Like Jarvis, I became an expert on the art as well as the manufacture of glass. Later, I purchased the technology and expertise I needed to be in the global market. New England's fuel became a major roadblock.

Magarac: What was the fuel issue?

Libbey: It was a lot like your oil problem today. Most of the glass houses of the 1850s were in New England. The only readily available fuel was hardwood, which was being lumbered out rapidly with a related increase in price.

England had lumbered out its forests decades earlier, and made the switch to more efficient coal. By the 1870s, the glass companies were moving to the coalfields of Pennsylvania and West Virginia. Europe had lumbered out its hardwood several decades earlier, and was running successfully on coal and coal gas. Coal was a cheaper and more efficient fuel. It was dirty, and ultimately we converted our plant to gas and oil. In the high-end art glass industry you needed clean environments to package in. Still even with the necessary additional cleaning, England had a cost advantage with coal. Many American companies transferred to coal without the investment needed to clean finished product. Customers did not want to open their package and find their cut glass covered with dust. Packaging is critical when you compete globally. The package needs to reflect the quality of the package. Many companies failed to break into the high end European market because of coal dust on the product. Europeans treated their glass as artwork, which took me several visits to fully appreciate. In the end, our success was born out of the fuel crisis.

Magarac: Do you think that your love of world art helped you form a global company?

Libbey: An excellent question; few have seen this link to my glass manufacturing. Even the low-end glass products are collectible and have attributes of art. This perception of art in our products was critical to our global success. We used artists and designers throughout our various companies. Even a simple water tumbler was designed as a piece of art. This led us into a re-awakening of colored glass in the industry. Some of these colored glasses helped us break into many European markets. Libbey Glass re-introduced ruby red to the Europeans and further developed colors such as peach, cherry, and creams. I targeted the global market when most thought it was a foolish venture to take on the established market.

Magarac: Even Adam Smith warned about taking on a nation's core industry. Do you think it is possible today for Americans?

Libbey: Not only possible, but necessary. California vineyards have used a similar model to mine to take on and succeed in the international wine market. It has taken years, but California wines are winning awards around the world. The vineyards are utilizing superior natural resources and reducing costs. I especially like what I see in the California olive oil industry. Here's a recent industry that is also utilizing California's natural advantage to take on the Mediterranean monopoly. Twenty years ago there were only six producers, but today there are over five hundred; mostly small, but operating in the high end of the market- "extra virgin" (Extra virgin being the first pressing of the best olives). While American producers account for less than one percent of the world market, they have doubled their market share over the last ten years. Their product is high quality and price competitive, but they lack a solid distribution system.

Magarac: How did you build a global distribution network?

Libbey: It was difficult. I started by touring the glass industry in Europe. Then I looked for potential alliances, which took time. The European market was tightly controlled, and I had to build relationships one at a time. Meanwhile, at my factories I had to be innovative and bring costs down. I spent a huge amount of money, more than the company had, (against the advice of my board of directors) to have a world-class exhibit at the World's Fair of 1893. Libbey Glass was near bankruptcy at the time. I dominated that fair and made Libbey Glass an international name. I built a complete factory to show our capability to produce art glass. I sent over a hundred glassmakers and artists to the fair to further prove the point. We took a Gold Medal in cut glass for our punch bowl. I hired Charles Barry, a proficient linguist in 15 languages, so we could get an international message to all visitors.

We made a special glass fiber dress for Infanta Eulalie, a Spanish princess. No one in the world had ever produced glass fiber. The princess and Royal family loved the dress and designated Libbey Glass Company as the official glass company of the Royal Family. In addition, millions visited the exhibit and our sales skyrocketed. The international market requires aggressiveness. The World Fair was a gamble, but it made Libbey a name known throughout the world. I followed up with a European tour to get outlets in Paris and London. It took years, but that network grew and by 1920, we had not only distribution, but also joint European companies. We were a major factor in many markets and products. You see the same thing with General Motors' slow but steady progress into the Chinese automotive market.

Magarac: Why do you think our import-export balance is so out of proportion?

Libbey: I don't think there is any one answer, but politics, labor costs, lack of aggressive technology investment, and the lack of a global mindset are part of the problem. Of course, I had all of these barriers, too. We had a major focus on product and technology. In many cases my interests functioned as an engineering or technology company. We leased our glass making machines over the world. We also sold exclusive rights and built alliances as well as joint ventures. Our corporate arrangements were always low key; it was not the giant American company Libbey, but a number of interlocked companies.

Of course, you have a fuel crisis as well, but high prices, not lower, will correct that. I saw this happen over and over, not only with hardwood but many things. Sperm oil lamps were the major source of lighting in my youth. Sperm whale price rocketed in the 1870s as it became scarce.

That price and shortage spurred a technology boom that resulted in kerosene production and the electric light. High price is one of the greatest motivator of innovation. The last thing you want is oil prices to be reduced. Many great industries have been born out of raw material crises.

Magarac: How did you handle your labor costs?

Libbey: The labor costs were problematic, even more so in the middle and lower end American market. I moved the company from New England to Toledo to get better fuel costs and some labor cost reduction. It was a difficult business and personal decision to leave Boston, but it came down to survival. I worked with the union, even transported them and their families to Toledo, but in the end I had to bring in new employees and change pay scales. Mike Owens was my manager, and he was tougher than me on addressing labor costs. Labor costs are part of the mix in global competition, but I believe marketing is just as important. Labor costs almost sent us into bankruptcy, but marketing pulled us from the brink. It wasn't until 1915 that my companies had a major labor advantage, and that came from automation, not negotiation.

In 1890, the labor costs of window glass production in the United States were three times higher than in Europe.[23] Within twenty years, we turned that around with the Colburn sheet machine. It took a painful flow of investments, and a lot of hard work to get that technical breakthrough. I might also add that the McKinley tariff protection allowed us to generate enough money and time for that revolution in glassmaking. I think often there has been a disconnect, between the responsibility of government and that of companies. In 1881, a Tariff Commission was formed to monitor and report on the industry with respect to effect of the tariffs. Many times my executives were in Washington

---

[23] Warren Scoville, *Revolution in Glassmaking,* (Cambridge: Harvard University Press, 1948), 241

more than Toledo, but this weekly give-and-take was good for the country. It assured that profits generated by the tariff resulted in improved wages and investment.

Magarac: So even as an international manufacturer you favor tariffs?

Libbey: Absolutely! Then as now, the greatest market in the world is the United States. The American market gave us the capital to invest and the money to pay good wages. The Tariff Commission oversight assured investment. The result of the tariffs from 1880 to 1915 is a matter of record. Wages and employment increased. There was a revolution in glassmaking; automatic glassmaking machines replaced centuries old practices. In addition, our exports soared. Just as important was that glass product prices were constant during the period.[24] The industry and government acted responsibly during the period. Our growth in global markets allowed us to keep prices down. Every government official, union leader, and executive should study period in the glass industry of 1880 to 1915. It shows what can be achieved in a balanced American economy.

Magarac: But didn't American tariffs hurt you in doing business in Europe and elsewhere?

Libbey: The answer is no, but to be fair, there were no multi-national trade groupings. Where foreign tariffs blocked our product sales, we sold the licenses, rights, and rented our improved technology. Better technology can never be embargoed! Countries need technology to stay in the game, and our tariffs produced that technology. The bottom line is that the best deal is to have the American market.

Magarac: What other factors played into these 45 years of growth and profits?

---

[24] Scoville, 265

Libbey: Let's look at things in order of priority. Technology and technology implementation was the main issue, but that required the willingness to invest and the needed profits. Those profits were, to a large degree, the artifact of the McKinley tariff policy. We also had favorable raw material prices, which remained steady during the period. I credit the motivation to capitalism. This period of technology growth, employment growth, profit growth, and stable product prices was born in an industry crisis. Accelerating fuel prices lead to new and cheaper alternative fuels. High labor costs lead to new technology and automation. Declining markets lead to market and product innovations.

Magarac: The most amazing thing to me is the behavior of the American government even with the parties of today?

Libbey: Yes, viewed through today, it is amazing. The McKinley Republicans were pro-tariff and pro-business, but also had a strong labor following. The Democrats were anti-tariff and business with a strong labor following too. The understanding that business growth meant wage and job growth, however, moderated the behavior. The Republicans maintained tariffs, but the Democrats with Republican support in Congress formed commissions to monitor the tariffs. At the time, these almost constant reporting requirements to congress were a pain, but I now see their importance. Congress pressured profits to be invested in the industry and watched for price increases. Overall, this created balance.

What I see today is adversarial and political fighting. You have lost sight of what is good for Americans as a whole. Jobs and wages depend on business and labor working together. Tariffs today, as in the 1920s and 1930s are political tools instead of economic tools. In my day, tariffs were economic only to protect core industries, balance trade, and level the playing field. Where they were over applied was a result of a belief that America and Americans were to get priority. It was a benefit and reward for the worker's contribution to democracy. The American government was not the world's trade regulator. Today, it appears that we are more likely to help some foreign country than the state of Michigan. This political role was only starting to surface in my day. Today you give priority to your

Chapter Five

Cooperative Advantage and Supply Chains

Vertical Integration and Supply Chains

Vertical integration was come out of vogue recently, but it still can have a place. Historically, great capitalists, such as Carnegie, Ford, and J. P. Morgan found much efficiency in vertical integration. Henry Ford had a passion for reduced inventory because he hated bankers. Henry had grown up with the business, and understood that inventory represented wasted cash reserves that might cause him to borrow. Ford correctly looked at inventory as a double tax on the business. First it is cash that does not earn interest, and second it can cause a cash shortage resulting in borrowing and an interest charge. Ford moved to vertical integration (owning parts and service suppliers) as a cash policy. In the 1920s, Ford purchased the Detroit, Toledo, and Ironton Railroad to save on freight costs and inventory. The Detroit, Toledo, and Ironton brought in most of Ford's supplies. With the purchase of the railroad, Ford cut the manufacturing cycle from twenty-two days to fourteen days. Eight days cut out of the inventory carried to assure uninterrupted production saved $60 million dollars.[25] In addition, Ford increased railroad productivity and wages.

Carnegie similarly used vertical integration buying railroads, iron ore mines, and coalmines to support his steel operations. J. P. Morgan argued that supply chain integration

---

[25] Henry Ford, *My Life and Work,* (New York: Doubleday, Page & Company, 1922), 175

offered huge improvements in costs and efficiency. Morgan forced supply chain cooperation through financial trusts with interlocking corporate directors. The Japanese and Chinese use similar banking and financial trust arrangements today. Ford, Carnegie, and even Morgan were correct, but they suffered from the propensity of humans to abuse vertical integration to destroy competition. We have paid a high price for that abuse. In globalization we are forced to compete against international trusts and monopolies with inefficient supply chains.

Vertical integration is often necessary to improve standardization, growth, and efficiency. In the early 1800s, the struggling large gunpowder company of Du Pont, was restricted by the various and un standardized wooden barrels. In addition, these wooden barrels were low quality. Du Pont built its own cooper shop and standardized barrel sizes, allowing for huge profits. Rockefeller faced the same problem in 1860s, in shipping barrels of oil from Pennsylvania to his Cleveland refineries. This confusion brought Rockefeller into the barrel business. He was able to standardize oil barrels known as a "Pennsylvania Barrel." The Pennsylvania 42 gallon barrel remains the industry standard even today.

Ford knew the advantage of well-managed logistics, and its impact on inventory. The Built-to-Order revolution of today is a mere extension of Ford's early principle. Dell Computer's supply chain logistics created a new market. It is a model that today's automotive manufacturers are looking at. Logistical speed allows for more competition and customization.

Today the problem of supply chain is that it combines strings of producers with logistics. In a vertically owned supply chain, you are dealing with a corporate entity. Ford and Carnegie were masters of the overall logistics, which is not true in independent supply chains. In a global world, Ford trucks don't compete with Toyota trucks, but the Ford truck supply chain competes with the Toyota truck supply chain. Problems anywhere in the supply chain can cause competitive problems. The supply chain must be managed for success. Integrated communications and scheduling becomes paramount. A supply chain must act as a separate entity while crossing many organizations. Software certainly allows this to a certain degree, that is, where schedules can be electronically linked. I believe that supply chains need some form of cross-company management organization to operate seamlessly. Some companies have monthly team meetings for critical supply chains. Managers and workers take on ownership as the chain crosses corporate lines.

Vertical integration may seem like the management solution, but vertical ownership brings its own problems as the American automotive companies have found out. Your in house supplier can become non competitive quickly in a global market and put you at a disadvantage. This is painfully evident with the automotive parts suppliers, where we see bankruptcies as business goes to China for cheaper employment costs. Some companies are choosing to build in China, therefore, adhering to the vertical integration strategy. In any case logistics and scheduling becomes even more complex. The situation requires a new approach to management. A supply chain manager and organization may well be needed. Like any organization, performance measures must be monitored for improvement. The newer impendent logistics companies are emerging to fill this function of supply chain management.

Still, if supply chains are really competing as many claim, then they need to behave like a single organization. There are times that a decision must be made for the good of the overall chain while one company may lose. For example, say a part design change can save the assembler five cents a unit. Forcing the design on the supplier at an increased cost of over five cents does not improve the overall supply chain. The top dog of the supply chain usually dictates the terms. What's missing is someone to make a decision for the overall good. Often inventory and scrap costs are pushed down the chain, which makes for fierce competition, but it also can be destructive on the chain. Chain link competition, as Edward Deming pointed out years ago, can actually destroy overall efficiency and profitability. Cooperation is needed and is what is lacking today.

Vertical integration was at the heart of Andrew Carnegie and John Rockefeller successes. Basically it means control of the raw materials to finished product. Our laws oppose it based on the early 1900s environment of corporate trusts and abuse. Many believe supplier competition brings prices down versus in house control, and this idea has become the cornerstone of our anti-trust legislation. It also became unfashionable in management circles as we started to talk of core competencies, yet it is necessary in the global environment to be vertically aligned if not integrated. We need to own our Chinese suppliers in the fashion of Henry Ford. If we are to be the king of the globe then we need to use a new set of rules. Vertical global integration will be needed, and offers a success strategy. International competition includes fully integrated supply chains as well as horizontally integrated corporations. Many times large American corporations are competing with mega supply chains that are government or financially controlled by other nations, not under our anti-trust laws.

Cooperative Advantage Drives the Global Network

Cooperation vertically and horizontally, with suppliers and customers, between union and management, and among nations offers one answer. Cooperative advantage is a key tool in globalization. It focuses on advantage over completion. In fact, competitors can gain through cooperation. One local example is industrial distributor, Durkin and Wise. Durkin and Wise is part of a national cooperative of independent, small distributors that allows them to purchase at lower prices and better control inventory. Locally they have another member in the cooperative, but the gain outweighs any small completive gain lost. Cooperative advantage can also be developed through supply chains. Many business analysts feel that real competition is between supply chains not individual companies. It is not uncommon in the automotive industry to demand higher (very costly) quality improvements even though the auto company cannot realize any direct benefit from it. This only pushes costs into the finished product and down the supply chain. The supply chain needs to cooperate not foster completion through the chain. Simple standardization of parts and/or sizes can greatly reduce the amount of tooling and tool inventory required. General Motor's reduction of brand models will result in this type of tooling savings.

The idea of cooperation offers huge benefits. Honda and General Motors pooling resources to develop a hybrid car show unique creativity among competitors. This applies to smaller companies as well, which might share development, marketing, even advertising. Similar companies can share inventory or even employees. Small companies can form local manufacturing communities, which can share technicians like machinists as well as pool inventories and gain purchasing discounts. Hospitals, for example, are doing just that sharing laboratories and doctors. Cooperative advantage does require a level of management creativity and analysis beyond simple competition.

I'm a blacksmith, a Pittsburgher, and metallurgist who laments the passing of the American steel industry. I grew up in the Steel City of old. I still write steel and Pittsburgh history as part of the grieving process. It is painful to travel around Pittsburgh; I loved the slag dumps of my youth and the sulfuric smell of prosperity. It is clear that the great American Industrial Revolution is over. The great industrial lions of America have been tamed. Carnegie was a globalist, but he believed the center of the globe was in his steel city of Pittsburgh. Andrew Carnegie had attracted my forefathers because it was in vogue to bring cheap labor to the factories where today we bring the factories to the cheap labor. To Carnegie, currency exchange rates factored little into his capital decisions. Today the currency exchange rate decides which country's factories run. Carnegie's clerks and accountants were limited to how far they could live; today employees live hours from work or often in another country. Even your drive thru McDonald's order may be processed via India. Technology tied the globe to cheap labor availability.

I' m also a global citizen, but I never signed up to be one, and I didn't start out as one. The globalization of manufacturing forced me to leave Pittsburgh and the steel industry. Ultimately, I made a career change as most of my industry moved to Japan, and I wasn't ready to put the family on the boat. With globalization steel's decline was a short journey of only 15 years. I was a manager of one of the oldest and largest mills in Pittsburgh (Jones & Laughlin-Pittsburgh Works). The decline had started in the early 1970s. Politicians came from both parties and turned up at the mill gates every two years. Even the ones the steelworkers elected soon forgot the promises. By 1980, Brazil and Japan were shipping in steel cheaper than we could make it even if every body worked for free. Labor would do nothing to compete and the cheapness of the global market prevented the application of tariffs. In 1984, we were at the end of this great steel mill's life that had employed at its peak over 18,000 workers, yet on the last day less than 300 were on hand to close the gate for the last time. After a hundred fifty years, iron production had ceased in the "Iron City." Within a few years, the area's second great mill, Aliquippa Works would experience the same end. Globalization is today part of our lives and for the employee, manager, and small business; there can be no running from it.

The first and hardest step is to accept it! Many of the managers of those mills moved on to the mills of Canton and Cleveland only to attend another closing party a few years later. We were the diehards, many of us had the education to get out, but we loved this industry and its lore of greatness. Neither political party is going to change the economic engine that started with Adam Smith in the 18th century. Taxes and incentives can help at least in the short run, but ultimately, only the most competitive businesses and employees of the world will survive. The unacceptable answer would be to lower our standard of living and wages. Long term even that would be an endless fight as cheaper and cheaper labor would be found on the global market. The last American to suggest we reduce our standard of living was then President Jimmy Carter. We need to be competitive in technology and flexibility. This answer applies to both the employee and employer. Success requires a hard look at several factors: technology, flexibility, and value. The methodology will require another change in perspective from competitive to cooperative advantage, which is a profound change politically and operationally.

Cooperative advantage offers a challenge to employees, employer, corporation, union, and nation. Cooperative advantage also requires a new social, cultural, and political infrastructure. Cooperating to gain advantage remains foreign in our aggressive, capitalist society, and infrastructure. The classic example is of two small town competing gas stations sharing a tow truck to save costs. Cooperation can mean savings being shifted through the supply chain for the best overall costs. For example, many times an end automotive customer might demand tighter tolerances than they need under the banner of better control and quality. The result can be increased costs throughout the supply chain. Cooperation throughout the supply chain is critical, and maybe in the future a type of quasi-overall chain management will be needed to assure competition. Competition within the full supply chain can be detrimental, but unfortunately competition not cooperation is the norm. Many hailed Social Darwinism as the cornerstone of capitalism. It was believed to be basic, but today even the biological sciences are finding more examples of evolutionary success based on cooperation versus competition.

Cooperative advantage requires a focus on technology, flexibility, and customer dynamics. Technology is the white knight of the highly industrial countries, but it must be applied correctly. Technology counters cheap labor, but it requires foresight and investment. The workers, not the management, best apply technology. An overlooked part of the technology is its proper selection and implementation. Technology costs and it must be applied efficiently. My own experience in consulting generated an example of this significant management problem. A business-consulting firm had twelve professional secretaries on staff in the late 1980s. These secretaries were highly productive using the new computer software for typing-*Word Perfect*. The management hoped for even further gains with the conversion to Microsoft *Word*. The shocking result was a huge drop in productivity. Talking to these secretaries after implementation clearly revealed the problem. Word Perfect allows these professional typists to use the function keys on the keypads to do things like cut and paste. Word for Windows required the use of the mouse, which actually slowed speed typists used to finger/keyboard interaction.

It's not just a management issue. Employees tend to avoid technology and training when it should be their first priority. Technology must be the first priority of today's global employees. It must start with selecting your employer based on factors such as education benefits and training opportunities. It is an unfortunate fact that the determining factor in job selection is often the pure dollar wage offered. The recent graduate given a choice of two will select one on a minor advantage in salary. In one case a graduate selected a company that offered $50 a year more but lacked educational benefits. This represents the mental model that doesn't put technology, education, and training on the same par as compensation. Management needs to cooperate also in the implementation of technology. Management needs to create a technological environment for learning. That includes making technology, such as computers, digital cameras, and other equipment available to the employee for use at work and home. Hobbies and clubs should be fostered to motivate and interest employees in technology. The learning process continues when the employee leaves the building and that is the secret to success. The Ford initiative in the 1990s of giving computers to all its employees is an example. The bottom line is that technology training and education is not an in house function.

Managers tend to worry about the availability of technology causing employees to "waste" time. In the earlier 1990s, I had a boss that limited managers' and engineers' access so they wouldn't waste time playing games. Today many companies worry about Internet usage, and it can be a problem. Employees, however, spending time surfing and paying bills is not a technology problem but a management problem. Such a waste of time is characteristic of organizational problems not technology availability. With motivation and discipline, availability of technology will advance the skills and knowledge of employees. Technology is a necessity for both the company and employee. Ford Motor realized this in the 1990s when it gave personal computers to its employees.

An Interview with Clarence Avery

Clarence Willard Avery (1882-1949) rose from being Edsel Ford's manual training instructor to a key lieutenant of Henry Ford. Considered one of the major contributors to the assembly line system, Avery also took the methodology to Ford suppliers. He organized Ford Glass and Ford's Northern Michigan Iron, Land, and Lumber Company. He applied Just-In-Time practices to assure suppliers could get up with the Ford assembly line. For a time, Avery was in charge of the Ford Village Industries, which was a network of auto parts suppliers in small communities. He played a major role in the design of the Model A. He was instrumental in bringing Lincoln Motor Company into the Ford family. Leaving Ford, Avery took over Murray Corporation, which became a major auto parts supplier. Magarac met him at the Milan, Michigan recreational center, which was a Ford Village plant that produced ignition coils in the 1930s.

Magarac: This is a beautiful site for a business.

Avery: That was the idea. This was one of Ford's 18 village industries, which were located in small rural communities, like Northville, Milan, Saline, and Dundee. These communities were located on small rivers in Southern Michigan. They were all water powered by huge waterwheels like the one there, and had formerly been grist or flourmills. It was an effort to integrate manufacturing in rural communities, using part-time farmers as laborers.

Magarac: Managers are again studying the unusual concepts; you pioneered in the Village Industries. Do you see any modern applications?

Avery: Many. Take a look at the Auto Alliance (Ford and Mazda) plant down the road at Flat Rock. It's built in a former Village Industry community, but there are deeper connections between the past and the present. This highly automated plant is the home to hundreds of robots, but also has a peaceful Japanese garden, the type of natural connection Ford wanted in his Village Industries. The cooperative management model of the plant is reminiscent of our informal system of management here at Milan. The uses of lean manufacturing and Just-in-Time practices really are similar to the Village Industries.

Magarac: So you see Just-in-Time practices as a Ford concept?

Avery: Absolutely! Even Toyota's Taiichi Ohno claims he "learned it all from Henry Ford's book." I have to wonder how America deviated from Ford's basic principles of Just-in-Time. "Ford expected only a 33-hour lapse between the mining of iron ore and the production of a car from the metal from that ore, he might rightly be called the Father of Just-in-Time."[26] In the Village plants we used a visual card system to move parts, which is today called the Japanese *kanban* system. Many of our ideas have yet to be fully exploited such as flexible labor.

Magarac: The labor base was novel, but didn't the UAW call it- "Industrial Feudalism"?

Avery: Ford was far ahead of his time, but I'm sure he didn't realize it. The main part of our labor force was part-time farmers, housewives, and divorced women. The workers had flexible and seasonal hours for the farmer labor component. Some plants built inventory to allow farmers to tend to the crops in the spring and summer. This type of cooperation with the community was part of Ford's vision. In fact, Henry Ford did have a vision of industrial feudalism much like that of Robert Owen in Scotland. Peter Drucker noted that Owen's New Lamark and some American utopian communities such as Shaker Village, Oneida, Zoar, and New Harmony were "the intellectual ancestors" of Ford's village industries. Clearly, these communities approached some tenets of an industrial utopia. Town women loved the ability to walk to work. Small farmers found the income to survive. The management was layered, but with fewer layers. Farmers were also in the managerial ranks. The atmosphere was informal and included recreational opportunities.

---

[26] Howard Segal, *Recasting the Machine Age: Henry Ford's Village Industries,* (Amherst: University of Massachusetts Press, 2005)

The village industries offered an incubator for the development of suppliers and new products. Ford experimented with soybean additives for paints and plastics. Plants such as Saline produced some of the first plastic parts ever. Ford inspired by George Washington Carver, wanted to find new uses for agricultural products. This was all beyond my interests. We did experiment with logistical methods, which was more interesting to me. Henry started to go overboard with his soybean research. I tired of his soy meals at his Fairlane home. Of course, I'm sure Henry is pleased today with ethanol and bio-fuels. It should also be noted that the overall application of village industries was very energy efficient. Workers got to the factory without expending much energy, and the factories use of waterpower made them very energy efficient.

Magarac: Could this type of part time labor arrangement compete with the industrialized system of your Rouge and Highland Park plants?

Avery: Yes. One example is the production of Model T engine valves at the Northville Village plant versus Highland Park. "It had taken 3.5 minutes and had a cost of 9.5 cents to make a Model T valve at Highland Park in 1920 versus 1.26 minutes and 4 cents at Northville in 1923."[27] The simplicity and standardized product allowed us to expand these village industries. We could fine-tune these village operations to act as assembly departments.

Magarac: Some consider you a process genius because of your role in the assembly line. Were you able to take continuous operations to all of your suppliers?

Avery: Certainly, we found success at most of our suppliers. Our assembly plants set a demanding pace for our suppliers.

---

[27] Drew Pearson, "Henry Ford Says Farmer-Workmen Will Build Automobile of the Future," *Automotive Industries,* August 28, 1924

Some, like the glassmakers, became bottlenecks to overall production. We started cooperative development programs with all our glass suppliers to develop better and faster technology. I was very successful in patenting a new glass making process that could keep up with our assembly. We called the process of converting our suppliers-"Fordized." I was the lead man in that effort. Our supply chain was the real restriction on the speed of car production for years. It was frustrating to see an assembly line stopped waiting for parts, but it was a common sight in the early days of the assembly. As you know many times we had to expand into parts manufacture to assure timely supply. We moved into glass, steel, paint, and subassemblies when necessary, and of course, our Rouge Plant was fully integrated.

Magarac: Do you think the advantages of assembly production can be sustained in a customized global market?

Avery: Yes, but you need to build in flexibility. Assembly lines need to have flexible tooling and the ability to change quickly. The same is true for the whole supply chain. When you start customizing, you start to overlap and branch supply chains out. Supply chains can also lose efficiency. It can be done, but you have to work differently. Suppliers need to be part of product development, which means you need long-term relationships. I think the lack of these long-term relationships is the bottleneck with the competitive model. A new product will require an investment of the whole supply chain and that takes commitment.

Magarac: It has been in vogue to strengthen the supply chain without moving into the actual management of it. This seems a little different from your approach. How do you see the need?

Avery: I think it is consistent, and more readily implemented than our approach. We wanted to spread our manufacturing techniques to our suppliers, as Toyota does today with its lean manufacturing practices. We were extremely successful in taking over and managing supplier industries, but we had some failures too. In the 1930s, our tire suppliers became a major bottleneck. First, strikes in the rubber industry caused many shutdowns at our assembly lines and then rising prices plagued us. It was a tough decision to move into the tire business, since Mr. Firestone was a personal friend of Henry Ford. We moved reluctantly into tire making with similar successes in process improvements that we had with the railroads, steel, and glass. We failed miserably in our effort to create rubber plantations using the same techniques. After pouring millions into plantations, rubber processing plants, and worker villages in South America, the workers ran us out after the plantations failed. Once Firestone got things under control, we were happy to turn the tire business back to him. Actually, with the exception of our Rouge Plant, we were happy to let our suppliers run their businesses. We needed consistent deliveries, product, and prices.

Magarac: You seem to have found little consistency by your many ventures into supply. Weren't you in charge of a lumber supply operation for Ford frames?

Avery: Yes. I managed the Northern Michigan Iron, Land, and Lumber Company for Ford. It started because Model T frames were made of wood, and we could not count on lumber companies to do it consistently. Still, like many things, Henry got his hands into the chemical aspects of the industry. Scrap wood was converted into chemicals and became a new product that of charcoal briquettes. It became a very profitable lumbering operation in its own right and Ford used it into the 1950s. In the early 1950s, it built all of the Ford wooden station wagon bodies. What we realized, like Andrew Carnegie in the steel industry, that your supply chain was the mark of success, not any one-assembly plant.

One of the forgotten men in the development of mass production was Fred Diehl, who was head of Ford purchasing. Diehl worked to synchronize purchasing requirements with our production schedule before computers. Diehl had instead an army of buyers and clerks, but he did an amazing job. Diehl was famous for working with and developing suppliers through the 1920s. Today, Ford continues to lead to supplier-assembly line coordination via computers. The timing is just as amazing, with seats being made in Monroe, Michigan and arriving on the Mustang assembly line within two hours. This type of electronic management allows the supply chain to behave like an internal department, which in turn extends the assembly process, making it a Just-in-Time operation.

Magarac: The auto industry talks a lot about cooperation and supply management, but the suppliers talk about price cuts, spiraling and costly demands, and bankruptcy. How did you manage your suppliers in order to stay competitive?

Avery: Diehl was extremely skillful and applied simple purchasing rules, which fit the idea of good supply chain management. He instructed his buyers to look for at least two suppliers and use competitive bidding. Buyers were instructed to go over all the details of the specifications and supply requirements to assure process capability. Diehl built trust with the Ford suppliers that allowed for openness, not seen today. The bids did include a breakdown of materials, labor, overhead, and profits. This type of sharing required the type of trust we had with Harvey Firestone. In return, the supplier was assured a profit, and volume pressure was not used as a weapon. Profits of the supplier were assumed to be a necessary part of the bid. The system was based on personal relationships. Schedule and production problems on both sides had to be communicated quickly. Diehl became known for his fairness and that made the supply chain function well.

Often today, demands of higher quality and lower prices are made unilaterally. True cooperation has lost out to competitive positioning. The volume also became addictive to the automotive suppliers. Suppliers are in co-dependent relationships versus symbiotic ones. Just- in–Time means keeping the inventory for the assembly plants. When it comes to suppliers, lean manufacturing and Just-in-Time are given lip service too often. The lure of big orders make suppliers think optimistically about their process capability.

Magarac: Sounds like you have a lot of good ideas for start-up companies?

Avery: The real lesson of our Ford mass production system was how we built our supply chain in the beginning. We had no choice, but to develop suppliers, since none existed that could immediately meet our production rates. We built companies and friendships along the way. Supply factors were on an equal par with the assembly production techniques in building Ford Motor Company. I believe small and medium size companies overlook the supply chain and that ultimately restricts growth. Successful retailers are well aware of the need to develop a supply chain. Suppliers should also see the need in developing new start-up companies.

The Dodge Brothers nurtured Henry Ford's young start-up company. The Dodge Brothers were the biggest manufacturer of car frames and parts in the world. Ford needed their frames and parts to enter the business and grow. The Highland Park plant was built near the Dodge Brothers Hamtramck plant. Dodge even reduced prices to help the growth of Ford. The relationship failed on a personal level, but it was the root of our success. Still any start-up company needs to assure that its suppliers can and are willing to supply.

Magarac: Men like Edward Deming have called the relationship key to supply chain management. I guess you would agree?

Avery: I certainly would. Supply chains compete both internally and externally. You are always dependent on your supply chain. It is really a team, but most companies see it as competitive supply. Competitive supply breaks down the trust needed. Many times we made and asked our suppliers to make sacrifices. That is exactly what is needed today. The real triumph of mass production was World War II because you had real cooperation in the supply chain. You also had Government and military overseeing the supply chains. I believe you said something like an independent supply chain manager, possibly a manager selected by the suppliers. Profit has to "manage" in the supply chain, so there is mutual gain. Our B-24 bomber plant at Willow Run was a massive consumer of material, and we had our purchasing problems. The government auditors kept us on the straight and narrow. We also had the various military Quartermaster Corps to deal with.

It sounds like a lot of control, but it was needed to assure a fair profit, a superior product for the military, and the best process technology. The control also allowed for internal conflicts to be resolved, for the overall good of the product.

Magarac: Any thoughts on global supply chains?

Avery: I believe there are hidden costs to obtaining the cheaper global prices. Transportation and late delivery can be large. We believed in short geographic chains because of lower transportation costs and ease of management. We see logistics companies fulfilling the role of supply chain manager in global chains. I'm just not a believer in adding geography as a factor in your business. Our village industries used part-time labor and were close to the assembly plant to achieve fast delivery and better costs. We also used immigrant labor, part-time farmers, single women, and inter-city residents at many of our suppliers to reduce costs.

Magarac: So you would support the Wal-Mart philosophy of using cheap inter-city labor?

Avery: Don't you think the residents of your hometown of Braddock would love to see Wal-Mart create hundreds of jobs? Capitalism starts with jobs, high wages evolve from success. People are getting ahead of the evolutionary process. Get the job creating business; work hard to make it successful, and then wages can increase. I believe our inter-cities could offer competition to countries like China. We looked for just such opportunities at my day at Ford Motor.

Summary

1. Use cooperation to achieve competitive advantage

2. Supply chains require cooperation and compromise to successfully compete

3. Profitability trumps the methodology or approach

Chapter Six

Making Quality Pay

The Quest for Quality

Quality is not free; it comes at a cost and deserves a price attached to it. The demand of auto supply chains to endlessly improve quality in return for endless price reductions resulted in bankruptcies. There's no honor in meeting Toyota's quality requirements and going bankrupt that's a lesson I learned the hard way. If your customer is not willing to pay for quality, then there is no reason to supply it. Phil Crosby argued in the 1980s that quality was free (the title of his book). The issue of the 1970s was a lack of craftsmanship, not quality. Craftsmanship is a given and needs to be considered fundamental to an operating business. Quality is a commercial attribute of a product or service that has value.

When firms invest time, people, and technology in improving quality, there should be a payback or a market for it. Customer should expect craftsmanship, but they should expect to pay for quality. Quality saves money throughout the supply chain and has marketable value. You manufacture or design a service to a specific quality level or levels; it's a business decision. The myth of the endless quest of the craftsman for quality is at the root of the problem. Even a craftsman produced at various levels for increasing price. Generally the craftsman had a standard level for quantity, and for a price moved up to the requests of higher paying customers.

American manufacturing became quantity driven after World War Two. Craftsmanship was sacrificed for higher production levels and the customer accepted the quality level turned out. The fact was that most American manufactured goods had little global market competition until the 1970s. Craftsmanship was lacking as a result of little competition. The market had built in an infrastructure to handle poor craftsmanship or low quality level. Sears and Roebucks created a business on product service and repair. Without competition, the consumer settled for repair service as part of the package. After all, Sears would come out and fix any appliance. There was a debate about planned obsolescence for the sake of the economy, but there was also a level of acceptance. As the marketplace opened up, acceptance waned. Foreigners segmented the market on quality levels. My experience with the Japanese confirmed that they targeted the American market by inspecting in quality levels. Cars going to the United States received specific inspections to assure only the best coming to America. Lower quality levels were diverted to lesser markets. I worked with Sumitomo in the 1990s on a similar approach to gaining the American Toyota business. The Japanese demonstrated an understanding of economics and quality. This is the same decision-making process early craftsman used.

I specifically use the term craftsmanship versus workmanship. Craftsmanship is a quality minimum standard imposed on workmanship. Lack of workmanship supposes the problem is with the worker. Poor workmanship implies laziness on the part of the worker. The minimum standard should be set by upper management, but it is usually tacitly implied in a vague way. Upper management avoids strong and direct definitions purposely, fearing a loss in production. Thus lower management and the workforce are permitted to workout out a compromise. Only once in my management experience was a clear standard set by upper management. It happened at LTV Steel during an effort to achieve Ford Q1 certification. The individual plants of Ford could black ball certification for low quality. Our quality was average but specific problems had caused problems at the assembly plants. Ford seriously told upper management of LTV that business might be lost. The result was something never seen in all my experience and the workforce's experience. A memo by the president of the company-demanding zero defects on Ford shipments saying nothing else was to be tolerated. It was posted in the plant; I wish now I would have saved this historic document.

LTV had invested millions in implementing statistical process control and training. The quality system was lavished with ancillary support. Several printers actually made millions as well as suppliers. An elaborate system of standards was developed, an army of additional process control employees was employed, and statisticians hired. Sumitomo of Japan was hired as process control consultants. Seven years of intensive implementation of an extensive system had not changed the quality at Ford. That memo changed things within weeks. Quality going to Ford was dramatically improved, and rejections dropped off as never seen before. I was amazed; a single memo had done something that a world-class system could not. The president had simply defined the level of quality and craftsmanship. The response was swift and overwhelming. It tells of a much simpler solution. Investing in a quality system was a copout by upper management. It showed commitment without stating a quality standard. The heart of all quality systems failure, such as statistical process control, six sigma, ISO 9000, and numerous others is a disconnect between the system and an upper management's determination to apply it to its fullest potential.

Manufacturing moves from Quantity

As market globalization took hold in the 1970s, the demand for higher quality levels arose. Repair service no longer had to be part of the consumer package. The problem was manufacturers searched somewhat frantically for the answer. One-week trips to Japan brought back solutions like statistical process control. Statistical process control was overapplied. Control charts became wallpaper. Statistical process control could not replace the need for upper management to set an environment for craftsmanship to have a priority. Upper management main interest in statistical process control was its "promise" of less inspection. Inspection took on a negative aspect and caused many an internal struggle in American corporations. The problem was and remains upper management. Upper management has the power to change direction, but hesitated because they realized an attached cost. Statistical process control has often been a disappointment because it is no substitute for corporate leadership.

After years of trying to implement statistical process control, I'm well aware of its limitations. It basically uses statistics to identify trends and out-of-control situations, but these are often visually evident without statistics. This is why machine operators and production workers saw control charts as merely additional work. Quality auditors on the other hand rated your plant based on "more is better." Statistical process control has many good tools for quality professionals, but part of the statistical process control mantra was that the operator needed to "own quality." This caused organizational frustration in many cases. Again the statistical techniques started to become the problem not the solution.

Why did statistical process control fail to achieve its full potential? First, it was a system solution versus a management solution, both were needed. Its other shortcomings were its complexity and lack of ownership by the workforce or quality control. In many large companies there was a process control department separate from the quality department that created more confusion. I literally walked out of an interview at Huffy Bicycle for Manager of Process Control, when the plant manager asked me why I wanted to waste my talents in such a position. This organizational lack of responsibility reflected the confusion of higher management. Upper management failed to realize that no system could solve a lack of leadership. Another problem was inspection was dempathized and even demonized by upper management. While Japan's use of statistical process control was overplayed, its powerful use of inspection and auditing was also overlooked.

One powerful statistical tool that of process capability is often not fully appreciated. Process capability looks that the actual level of quality being produced and compares it to the customer demands. When you are not capable, it makes economic sense not to pursue the business. Upper management many times overruled the cold statistical facts pushing for performance results that the process was incapable of. Often you can inspect, cajole, and monitor success short run, but long run the statistical process capability applies. Many companies in the 1980s lacking process capability were able to "manage" short run success to gain the business. Once that was achieved, lack of process capability bankrupted them.

The beauty of statistical process capability is that it evaluates the current status of men and machine to satisfy a customer. It sets a benchmark for improvement. It is a management tool and a measurement of process efficiency. Conceptually it can be reduced to a single number for tracking, but improving it depends on training, improved standards, higher skills, better technology, and better equipment. Thus it is not a daily measure or even a monthly measure, but more biannual. It does not reflect quick fixes but management commitment to long-term improvement. Companies that never show improved process capabilities over years are problematic. Upper management should be compensated by their record on process capability. Process capability on key product attributes should be reported in the annual report. Profitability without process capability must be short run.

A definition of process capability is the ability of a process, service, or operation to meet customer's specifications or requirements. Numerically a number of greater than one implies a process is capable, at least, potentially. Statisticians use a further refinement known as Cpk process capability, which measures not only potential but also the ability of a process to meet that performance. Mathematically the difference is how you measure the performance of the process statistically. The potential capability uses the six-sigma variation of a process, which reflects the normal distribution. In calculating Cpk, half of three sigma of the normal is used plus the lower and higher end of the customer specification. Once again greater than one is the numerical goal for process capability. For the practical manager, you want Cp and Cpk to be greater than one. If Cp is greater than one but Cpk is less than one; it means the process is potentially capable, but it is not centered. To simply it, you want Cpk to be greater than one. When it's less than one then you need to find out way. See the appendix for a more detailed description.

Ideal Process Capability-Cp

Process Capability = $\dfrac{\textbf{Customer Specifications or Requirements}}{\textbf{statistical performance of the process (6 sigma)}}$

Six Sigma

Six sigma is a breakthrough approach, which has roots in Juran's "Diagnostic Journey." It is built on the fundamentals of statistical process control. One of its strongest points is it is based on process capability. Six sigma also builds on the team approach of earlier quality movements. Like statistically process control it requires extensive training in statistical tools and techniques. Another strength is its basic focus on goal setting and measurement. The power of goal setting alone can overcome a lot of weaknesses. Six sigma has plenty of them too.

One problem is six sigma over promises. Breakthroughs rarely come without cost, and that is what most companies are looking for. Six sigma looks for breakthroughs in process management, which is difficult. These ten to fifty fold improvements are more common with technology and equipment upgrades than process management. Six sigma teams are trained to go after high impact project, tackling the big problems versus the little ones. A lot go for the "big one" that has plagued the company for years. The problem is the "big one" is typically not a process management issue, but a machine or technology issue. These employee teams rarely have the engineering and technology resources to resolve it.

Project selection becomes paramount. The masters of breakthroughs such as Thomas Edison and George Westinghouse took months and even years to select projects with breakthrough potential. Six sigma does focus on project selection in its approach, but the emphasis is on breakthrough potential. There needs to be a focus on its potential to be resolved from process management. If the team is going to chase the "big one" then team makeup must be considered. Engineers and maintenance need to be included so in the event it's a technology issue; a proposal can be made for the need.

Another problem can be the nature of the employee teams. Generally they are temporary and trained in statistical techniques. Teams that function outside the normal company structure can be problematic. The team often will tend to find a solution for a department such as maintenance or engineering, which were not part of the team. My own experience with teams was that there was a tendency to look at incoming quality or incoming services or components. A team project should limit its scope to the area over which they exercise control or build a diverse and cross-functional team.

Getting the most out of Six Sigma

1. Project Selection

Select medium level fruit that is projects that can improve on process capability permanently. Include an accountant on the team to assess project potential and cost of implementation. Focus on a process management project unless you are specifically looking for new technology applications. Project should have approval of upper management.

2. Team Selection

Teams should be very diverse and cross-functional. The best examples of breakthrough teams are in the aircraft industry using matrix management. Matrix management was cross-functional. Team members should be selected by department or area management to help ownership and buy in. Do not create a six-sigma infrastructure of a separate organization, this destroys company wide ownership. Teams should include and represent the various organizational groups such as maintenance, accounting, customer service, sales, etc. Suppliers and/or customers should be included based on the nature of the project.

3. Scope and Constraints

Scope and constraints such as implementation dollars and technology dollars should be clearly defined for the team. Management must be involved in guiding the team. Many times management experience can be important in evaluating the potential of a project.

4. Compensation

Team members should receive some form of additional pay based on working on the project not on its success. Bonuses based on the project success are dangerous because the team menbers will be getting ideas from all employees. The team are not the innovators but facilitators of innovation. If the project is highly successful then a bonus to all area employees should be considered instead of the team alone.

5. System Complexity

Six Sigma needs to be tied into ISO 9000 to assure process improvements are monitored for process interactions in the process and supply chain.

Lean Manufacture

Lean manufacture is similar to six sigma, employee teams, and statistical process control but more focused on process management. Inventory issues are commonly addressed by in lean manufacture. The approach was developed from process improvement programs such as those of Toyota. This process focus and diverse approach has led to newer programs such as "lean six sigma." Lean manufacture has lacked the technique approach of six sigma, so it is a logical combination. Lean six sigma leads to a more integrated approach.

ISO 9000 and TS 16949

ISO 9000 and its automotive counterpart TS 16949 are system standards for manufacturing products or creating services. The standard supplies a basic foundation for process management. Being certified assures that the system is in place. ISO is a well-conceived standard developed by international experts. It has the same inherent weakness of other programs when is upper management delegates its responsibility to the system. I have personally implemented ISO systems at over 60 companies, and for most, it was a system without teeth. The fact is that I can get a company certified without a truly functioning system! I still personally believe that a forceful well-communicated standard of craftsmanship is more powerful than any system. The real power is in combining a management standard of craftsmanship with an operating system standard. ISO's stated goal is to do just that.

ISO offers some very worthwhile process components. The corrective action and diagnostic loop can be used to the advantage of many, but commitment is needed. The use of standards can also be powerful, but most companies overdo this. Standards need to be simple and concise, like an instruction manual. The requirement for goals and objectives represents a common and foundational component of any process control system. The review meeting requirement is excellent but should be held every month, not biannual. The requirement to review the process capability before taking an order is meritorious and needed in most companies. The requirement to track quality parameters, delivery, supplier performance, and customer feedback are again foundational and necessary. The emphasis on inspection in ISO is refreshing in a post-Deming world. Calibration also gains a much-needed focus.

The problems are numerous as well. While not a requirement, paperwork is over done in the implementation of the standard. The emphasis is more on form than results. While auditors interview management for commitment more is needed. There should be a grueling deposition of management under oath! Having the system means nothing unless management uses it as a way of life. The mission statement requirement does not get to the real point. The CEO or owner should be asked for a vision statement, then the auditors should look for evidence of its application. The CEO should be questioned extensively on corrective action and trends. Employee interviews by the auditor should be tough and probing. The emphasis should not be certification, but identifying system and commitment issues. The pass requirement should not be the number or magnitude of system non-conformances, but only that the company corrects all points noted, and corrections verified through re auditing the company. The cycle should be every six months.

Integrated Approach

Using the best and common components of ISO, TS, statistical process control, six-sigma, and lean manufacture, an integrated approach emerges.

1. Corporate vision

Written or unwritten vision is the key to success. The system for process control should reflect this corporate vision. Corporate leadership on the process system should be absolute and dominating. Henry Ford remains the best example of this. Mission statements should be a simple statement of the vision –ideally using less then seven words. The vision should set the standard of craftsmanship desired.

2. Objectives and goals

Objectives and goals should be set on an annual and monthly basis and tracked. A management review meeting should go over progress monthly. These goals should benchmark a minimum of measure of internal quality, delivery performance, customer feedback, an external measure of quality, status of corrective actions, inventory measures, and productivity. This allows for a balanced scorecard.

3. One sentence standards where needed

This should be coupled with employee training and, where necessary, an instruction manual. Standards must reflect the actual process used, not some engineering ideal. The over writing of standards is a major weakness in ISO implementation.

4. Corrective action

Corrective action and documentation of action should be the foundation of an operating system; here the ISO system can be a guide, but keep it simple.

5. Process Improvement and Technology Review

Technology review should be part of process improvement. Monthly focus meetings are necessary. Have an overview committee as well as teams, but avoid creating a new infrastructure. The great success of John Rockefeller was the use of committees for improvement and overview. These committees should not be employee teams but teams of employees. The makeup of the committee should be balanced with both workers and managers but selected by management. Process control is not self-directed.

6. Diagnostic Inspection

Inspection should be a priority throughout the system including raw materials receiving. Inspection feedback is central and should be done on a shift basis. Inspection has no value other than to correct the process. Inspection should be integrated into the process.

7. Quality Control Functions

Calibration and measuring device maintenance is fundamental for any system. quality control functions should be integrated through employee selection, training, and mission.

8. Supplier Programs

Active supplier programs should be ulitilized, not the passive approach of ISO. Suppliers should be brought in for annual goals. Supplier ratings should be sent out monthly even if they are qualitative.

9. Process Overview and Change Documentation

Process changes and there effects are controlled and monitored with the discipline of ISO 9000. Process changes represent the major source of quality problems. Change must be made with the full cooperation of the supply chain.

An Interview with Thomas Edison

Thomas Edison (1847-1931) is one of America's geniuses. He is known as the "Wizard of Menlo Park." His New Jersey research compound was named. Thomas Edison considered himself a professional inventor, best known for the electric light bulb, but the holder of over 3000 patents. Other inventions include the phonograph, stock ticker, storage battery, motion picture camera, as well as over a hundred electric devices. Both Henry Ford and Charles Schwab idolized Edison, and he remains today an inspiration for America's youth. Edison thoroughly researched the economic potential for any project before launching his research efforts. With the exception of the electric light, he set deadlines for the completion of his projects. Menlo Park, which today has been relocated to Greenwich Village, was truly an invention factory. Tom Magarac interviewed him at his birthplace of Milan, Ohio, now a restored historical site.

Magarac: Sorry, I missed you at The Henry Ford in Dearborn.

Edison: I, like Henry, still haunt my old Menlo Park buildings there. It's home to my chemical collection, which was my love and passion. Henry had a tough time getting me to donate that collection; it was the last earthly possession to give up.

Magarac: Visiting the Menlo Park was indeed inspirational! As I look for ways to make America competitive, I feel some answers lie in your old compounds. We don't see the type of breakthrough inventions that came out of your Menlo Park. Why do you think that is?

Edison: It was our goal to have a breakthrough invention every six months. We were in the business of invention, which resulted in a pragmatic focus. I loved science, but left the theoretical research to the scientists. I wanted to apply science and make practical inventions. By 1870, the advance of science was far ahead of its practical applications. You need a project and a time goal to be successful; the rest is just backbreaking work.

Magarac: Six Sigma today tries to achieve that type of breakthrough focus.[28] Still, many companies have not gotten the large gains hoped for. Some believe the problem is that the projects do not have breakthrough benefits. How did you develop so many breakthroughs?

Edison: What is often overlooked about my work is that I thoroughly researched a project for its payback and feasibility before launching the project. I learned that from my first invention of the vote recorder for legislative bodies.

---

[28] Six Sigma is a process improvement methodology developed by Motorola Corporation in 1987. It searches for breakthrough improvements in process control, quality, and delivery. Over 800 major companies have tried some of the methodology with varying degrees of success.

The vote recorder fit my background in telegraph work, and I developed it in a relatively short period, receiving a patent in 1868. It was mechanically a great device, able to record votes and individuals. I took the machine to the head of the Congress's Chairman of Committees, and he was impressed. The problem was however, he did not want to reduce delay, which he felt was part of the legislative process. This inability to market a "successful" invention changed my view not only of success but project selection. Looking back, even if I had sold it to the US Congress and all the state legislative bodies, I probably would have barely broken even. I decided to invent things that could make me money.

I considered myself, a professional inventor with limited time. I needed something I could bring to market quickly. In addition, I needed a market! After the inability to market the vote recorder, I left penniless to New York to take a job at Gold & Stock Telegraph Company, which used the telegraph to get stock quotes to thousands of customers. That was a market and the technology needed to exploit it was in place. Within six months, I had a "Universal Stock Printer," which would become known as the stock ticker. Within a few more months, I sold the rights for $40,000 (about a half million today), and also started a manufacturing plant to produce them. More importantly, I used the money to start an 'invention factory." I learned to research projects for their potential and payback. Project selection is more important than the improvement itself.

Magarac: I see your point, but shouldn't companies look for ways they can make improvements?

Edison: Well, a company makes a large commitment in capital and resources when a team is put together. You need to have a large impact to cover the effort. Many companies today use six- to- ten people teams to work on process improvements, without considering better methods for project selection. Too many times, these teams go after what you call "low hanging fruit." Of course, the other problem is the team goes after the biggest and oldest problem, spending years in an unsuccessful effort.

Six-Sigma's roots goes back to the diagnostic problem solving of Juran. Juran argued for a breakthrough approach to problem solving. You need to stretch people and resources to achieve high performance. I truly believe we suffer from setting our goals too low in problem solving. The danger is that a lot of times home run hitters don't have good batting averages. A home-run hitter is most likely a very different type of hitter than the solid average hitter. Organizations need to train for home run hitting breakthroughs. Breakthroughs are major jumps in process improvements.

Magarac: So you believe in avoiding the big hitter?

Edison: Not necessarily. My greatest reward came from my greatest challenge- electric light. I really got into electrical lighting late in the competition. Electric bulbs had already been patented (although not very efficient). Gas lighting was the real competition and electrical distribution was the real problem. I reviewed this project for over a year before jumping in. " I bought all the transactions of the gas engineering societies, etc. and all the back volumes of the gas journals. Having obtained all the data and investigated gas-jet distribution in New York by actual observations. I made up my mind that the problem of the subdivision of the electric current could be solved and made commercial."[29] In addition, I researched all the experiments done on lighting devices and tested a few on a laboratory basis.

My financial analysis suggested I would need a huge amount of money to launch the effort. I was able to get some financial backing from J.P. Morgan and the President of

---

[29] Edison quote, Ronald Clark, *Edison,* (New York: Putman & Sons, 1977), 89

Western Electric. I realized this was to be the main project of my newly started research facility at Menlo Park. In a two-year period it was really the only project of an eighty-man operation. I had to hire specialists, such as glassblowers and electricians. If you go big then it must have the organization's total backing of resources and money. Even with all we had, it took us years with failure after failure. If you look at my vote recorder, stock ticker, and electric lighting as projects, the sweet spot for six sigma teams is stock ticker projects. The vote recorder lacked economic impact, and electrical lighting systems were too long term.

Magarac: Certainly, that approach makes project selection paramount?

Edison: Project selection is everything. You need to pick battles big enough to affect the outcome of the war, but small enough to win. I made costly mistakes, but I learned. Still, I had a hard time letting go of some projects. At Menlo Park, we were typically running eight to ten projects with six to eight men teams. We had to be successful or we lost money. Product and process improvement is costly, and you can't waste your resources on projects that lack large paybacks. Select the project well and then assemble a strong team. "The way to do it is to organize a gang of one good experimenter or what you would call a project manager and two or three assistants, and appropriate a definite sum yearly to keep it going. Then you send all the related publications and patents to them to review. Finally, let them experiment continuously."[30] My job was to review progress and costs. The teams were free to use the extensive library, get supplies from the storeroom, and use the machine shops.

Every day I checked on the project teams and adjusted resources if needed. Top management needs to select the project, select the team members, and monitor

---

[30] Edison quote from William Pretzer, *Working at Inventing,* (Baltimore: John Hopkins University Press, 1989), 60

progress. Today, team building for morale and project management get confused. In a lot of ways I needed experts, not creative genius. In fact, many geniuses like Nicola Tesla, left me for Westinghouse's research efforts. I built teams on their expertise and how it could help the project success. Project work was hard, dog work with little room for individual creativity. Individual creativity can at times interfer with project work.

Magarac: You mean there was only room for one Edison?

Edison: Exactly! Project management is the responsibility of top management. They have the best view of the organizational needs. I disagree with the six-sigma approach and Westinghouse on this point, which had a collaborative approach even in project selection. I have no problem with brainstorming for potential projects, but ultimately, the decision must be at the top.

Magarac: Cost would seem to be an impediment to innovation?

Edison: Not really, all innovation comes at a cost. In 1890, I started a major project for the economical processing of low-grade ore. I spent too many years on the project, which drained my personal funds. I sold General Electric stock, ultimately losing control of the company. I invested too much. After five years, I found the key, but a rich ore deposit in Minnesota made my process uneconomical. It cost me in excess of $6 million and most of my General Electric stock ownership.

After that, I implemented a systematic accounting method for my invention factory. Hours were correctly assigned to the projects, and costs were reviewed weekly. Both material and labor costs were tracked. Project potential and progress were reviewed monthly. This is what I like about the Six-Sigma approach; it incorporates lessons that were extremely costly to me. Project potential can change just as costs. At times, and I known this is hard personally, you need to cut your losses and move on. It's a tough management decision because success is also dependent on determination and commitment. Still, we needed a breakthrough project every year to stay in business, and we had finite resources. When you over commit your resources to a project, it is not the actual costs, so much as the opportunity costs that hurt you.

Magarac: Why do you think so many teams today fail to achieve breakthroughs?

Edison: The teams lack focus, management, and direction. Self-directed teams lack the focus needed. I selected the projects, then formed the team, and therefore I played the role of top management. I made project selection a top management responsibility. Today, you delegate this to the team. I built my invention factory on the crafts model, and I was the master craftsman. Project selection should not be based on team morale, but corporate mission. I used picnics, late night sing alongs, and baseball games for morale. Top management must be involved in project selection if you want breakthroughs. Many criticized me for my autocratic methods, but I was not running a corporate R&D center. If you want a model for corporate research talk to George Westinghouse. I was overbearing and demanding of my teams.

Actually, I never used the term team, I preferred gang. Gang was the term used in the glasshouse for the master glassblower's working group. I looked at project development as a craft. My teams were groups of artisans, and few were cut out for this type of work. A project was an experimental campaign. I think top management needs to build the team to meet the project objectives. This is different than what I see happening today. You need not only expertise in problem solving but specialized skills as well. A team may need maintenance, accounting, engineering, or other specialized knowledge to be successful. These are the factors top management needs to consider in building teams. A project team should always have two levels of expertise, the experimental craftsman and the specialized expert. Project management is much different than the management of creativity. George Westinghouse had a creativity factory, mine was an invention factory. They produced much different products.

Magarac: You didn't believe much in college-educated engineers?

Edison: And that gets to the difference between George Westinghouse and me. I needed specific expertise for my projects such as glassblowing or accounting, not theorists or creative engineers. Electrical engineers got bored with my directed and endless experiments. Again, I wasn't looking for new ideas, but project success. The ideas were mine. Westinghouse on the other hand was constantly looking for new ideas. Projects are not research ideas but development. I lost the war of currents because Westinghouse came up with creative ideas such as alternating current while I was developing direct current applications. But most of my success was in development work that was my strength. Process improvement is more developmental than research. Of course, I needed some college-educated graduates. I hated math and hired a mathematician to do my calculations.

Magarac: What do you like in the Six-Sigma methodology?

Edison: I especially like the idea of training a skilled experimenter. The green and black belts are trained in problem solving skills and statistical analysis. This fits my concept of invention as a craft performed by craftsmen. I tried to develop the same skills for my master experimenters and project leaders through project experience. I had a pool of master experimenters as well as, expert machinists, glassblowers, and other specialized experts.

The other emphasis I like is that of metrics and goals. Measuring progress is fundamental to project management. I required project notebooks to be maintained and left on the workbench. As part of my daily rounds, I would check and read these notebooks every day. These notebooks, along with the labor accounting system, allowed me to monitor progress.

Magarac: But Nicola Tesla said you lacked methodology and preferred to look for a needle in a haystack, when a little science could greatly reduce the size of the stack?

Edison: I fair criticism, but what I lacked in methodology, I made up for in drive to achieve the goal. My science was good, but old line. My success, however, points to the fact that metrics trump methodology!

Magarac: Of course, Six-Sigma is a process improvement methodology, but what application do you see for product development?

Edison: I worked with both product and process development at Menlo Park, but my love was product invention. Product invention has a final phase beyond that of solution verification in process improvement. With the electric light, once I found the proper filament, I still had a long way to commercial development. "All the means to set up and test more deliberately every point of the electric light, so as to be able to meet and answer or obviate every objection before showing the light to the public or offering it for sale either in this country or in Europe."[31]

Magarac: That's FMEA?

Edison: FMEA?

---

[31] Thomas Edison to Theodore Puskas, November 13, 1878

Magarac: Failure Mode Effect Analysis, which is used to improve both product and process by looking at potential means of failure to design.

Edison: FMEA is then necessary for product development, and I used that type of methodology on all my inventions. It can work well in process improvement too. The issue is that the process FMEA rarely leads to a breakthrough. Remember, by your own definition a breakthrough is a 2X to 10X improvement. In this respect, I see it more as a process control method versus process development. I see it as a plant engineering function, not a breakthrough project technique. Still, even process improvement requires looking at the modes of failure. In breakthrough project management simple cause and effect analysis can be used.

Magarac: How did you motivate your teams? Money? Rewards?

Edison: The satisfaction of project success. Pay at Menlo Park was almost non-competitive, yet many offered to work without salary to be part of it. The hours were terrible, usually a 60-hour week with Sunday off. The work was tedious and boring. These men were special. Many left after three months. I did maintain a core, which you would call project managers. Probably, one of the few benefits was flexible hours. Teams tended to work at night with daylight hours off. Most of the employees were young and single. Considering today's labor market, I would not recommend my employment practices. Still, payment for improvements is a dangerous thing. Improvement comes from passion, not motivation.

Consider one of my best lead experimenters, John Lawson. He lacked experience but had the passion. In a simple letter he wrote, "I care not what the work is if I can only have a chance to study. I wish to become a chemist. Had I the means I would devote myself to chemistry. I'm willing to do anything, dirty work- become anything, almost a slave, only give me a chance to pursue the studies that I love." Now that's the type of passion you need to seek out. In the tough road to a breakthrough, you need passion to sustain you. You can't pay people enough for the type of work demanded.

Magarac; How do you feel about the use of statistical process control in project management?

Edison: I like the use of statistics in experimentation, but I believe you put too much hope in statistics to replace old-fashion experimentation. Maybe I'm a bit behind the times here, but I've seen companies struggle with statistical process control as they are today. These programs appear to be middle or bottom driven. You want top management support, but no team involvement. Another issue is trying to make everyone a statistician. I hated and avoided math, but realized its use. I hired professional mathematicians. Statistics is a powerful tool in the hands of an expert. When a team must tackle a difficult experimental design, then a statistical expert should be assigned to the group. I would have one professional statistician with software experience at every plant. A four to six week trained black belt lacks the real expertise in this science. If you are going to use this science, you need to hire the real expertise.

One simple statistical tool I like is the Pareto chart. Its allows you to analyze where to put your focus, money, and resources when aiming for breakthroughs, requiring the highest potential projects. I also like the simple fishbone approach for cause and effect.

Magarac: Would you change the nature of black belt training?

Edison: Yes, you need project managers, not statisticians. I'd be more selective when deciding who becomes a black belt. Again, you need leadership skills coupled with determination. These Six-Sigma projects can tie up huge amounts of dollars and time; you need the best people managing them. Your present system gives you analysts versus project managers. You need to use the model of matrix management used in the aircraft design industry and by engineering firms. When you select a specific project, management needs to spend some time selecting the right project manager for the job. Project managers have different expertise and experience, and it's management's role to make the right match.

Magarac: So you think project management is the real issue, not the black belt, statistical methodology, and Six-Sigma structure?

Edison: Alfred Chandler, a business historian, said structure follows strategy. Even, Henry Fayol believed objectives, resources, and requirements determined structure. Apple Computer unorthodox structure is similar to Menlo Park. How the project team is selected, organized, and managed is a function of objectives and resources. In its early days at Motorola, Six-Sigma lacked the structure of today. I think as the infrastructure evolved, Six-Sigma became less effective. When you're spending a lot of money and time on infrastructure, you have gone too far.

Also as professional trainers and consultants got into the act, Six-Sigma started to become a collection of previous process control initiatives. Trainers rolled in statistical process control, FMEA, team building, Design of Experiments, TQM, cost of quality, etc., and also new job titles, such as champion, process owner, green belt, black belt, and master black belt. In addition, Six-Sigma became very quality oriented sometimes over looking other opportunities. Many consultants just put a new title page on their old materials. Companies are investing years in training before they ever get to practical projects. These trends have weakened the flexibility of Six-Sigma, so successful in the early days at Motorola. Menlo Park teams were flexible in all aspects except commitment to the project objective.

Magarac: So you feel all the training is unnecessary?

Edison: Train by project work and improve skills through experience. Six-sigma is too long on training, and too short on leadership.

Magarac: Finally sir, I have to ask if you think companies should use your power nap approach?

Edison: Lots of companies are! Creativity is exhaustive, just like physical exercise.

Chapter Seven

Automation, Non-Linear Systems, and Robotics

Sensemaking

Automation is not an end in itself as too many managers look at it today. After all, we are in a "new era", a new economic paradigm, and the post Industrial Revolution. The problem is that we have more technology than can be managed more often than not. My premise addresses this head on. Information and technology have increased the need for strong middle management has also increased. The interface of man and technology has always been a fiction point from the earliest days.

Jules Verne in the 19th century struggled with man and technology in over thirty of his books. In the 1950s, Norbert Wiener coined the word *cybernetics* to look at management in an automated world. Wiener was prophetic in many aspects of the post Industrial Revolution. He foresaw the problem of information overload, entropy systems, and technological abstraction. Wiener developed these concepts in two famous works – *Human Use of Human Beings* (1950) and *Cybernetics*.

Let's look at information overload. Wiener put it in scientific terms – "When there is communication without need for communication, merely so that someone may earn the social and intellectual prestige of becoming a priest of communication, the quality and communicative value of the message drops like a plummet". Wiener, long before the information overload of today, foresaw the issue of communicative value. More information is not better. Anyone trying to research in the Internet understands this. Idealists see the Internet allowing flatter organizations with more direct communication. The problem is that there is nothing to maintain communicative value, let alone improve it. Information needs to be sorted and diverted. It is here that we see the increasing role of middle management with information and technology.

Wiener's other insight was that overall operating systems of any type are entropy; that is, they naturally decay. This is the organizational corollary of the second law of thermodynamics. Information also becomes obsolete. The cybernetic component known as feedback is needed to steer the operations. Middle management is the tactical feedback control that adjusts and corrects the operating system. Wiener noted that in battle, information became obsolete in hours. Like the centurion of old, the middle manager must take over both the strategic and tactical role in the heat of battle. Again technology as we will see, increases the need for middle management.

System entropy and communicative value are part of a larger issue known as technology abstraction or "sensemaking". Sensemaking became a term of interest in the 1970s after Three Mile Island's nuclear accident. The suggestion was that operations and managers were so removed from the operations that they could not fully sense what was going on. The warning signals and computer alerts overwhelmed them. The problem grows today as more operations are controlled and managed via computer screens. The issue is not day-to-day control but decision points, warnings, etc. The process can no longer "make sense" to the decision-maker. Sense is both in the computer as well as the actual process.

Wiener envisioned Sensemaking as technical abstraction. This abstraction occurs at all levels even at the point of operator/process interference. Younger pilots in high tech jets report a lack of reality, as it appears to be a video game. Sensemaking is a serious challenge to operations management. It's an area that will require more and more of middle management attention. I saw the same thing in automated process control panels. As a manager of a highly automated steel processing plant, I often walked into the control pulpit with red lights glaring on endless panels. The operators when questioned about the red warning lights could tell me why they were false signals from thier experience. They often had a rubric of checks of other indicators, which better analyzed the reality. Much of this was knowledge, hard earned, and experience that was not readily transferable. This type of sense making can only be learned by simulation. The random nature of processing problems requires the type of critical thinking that comes from experience, and the best way to gain that experience is simulation. Since Nine Mile Island, nuclear power plants do monthly simulation training like pilots.

Another part of sensemaking is to make today's information overload and turn it into a usable resource. Peter Drucker said of middle managers – "they're similar in function to boosters on a telephone cable, which collect, amplify, repackage, and send information". Technology has, in many ways, caused disorder out of increased information. I know many times I would start to research something on the internet, only to be confused and frustrated two hours later by overload.

Non-Linear Systems and System Complexity

Systems after the application of Ford's assembly line and Michael Owens's continuous process of batch products are no longer linear. Changes in the process, therefore causes interactions at various levels. A simple improvement change at one step of the process can result in a negative change somewhere else in the process. This is why TS 16949 requires notification when a supplier in the automotive supply chain makes a change. Changes must be documented and monitored because of these interactions. Often a change made to the right reason causes a major problem unexpectedly upstream. Some of my great management challenges came from improvement process changes causing disasters. We will see that system complexity requires more middle management control, not less. We are dealing today with the broader term of *Flow Technology*. Flow technology is longer the linear approach of early pioneers such as Henry Ford.

This system complexity is difficult to manage. Change must be managed and the responsibility lies with middle managers. It also requires organizational discipline that can be found in ISO 9000 or TS 16949. We can no longer assume a simple change is linear affecting only one variable in the process; furthermore, the whole supply chain process has to be considered. For example, as a steelmaker, I once made a simple change to improve the quality of axle steel for General Motors. The improvement didn't seem to require notification of GM, other to tell them they would be receiving better quality. In fact, their incoming inspection confirmed they were getting higher quality steel. They were getting cleaner steel, but the heat treating characteristics were also slightly changed (a result, we at the time were unaware of). The heat-treating change caused a problem in the heat treatment process of the axle, which increased brittleness of the axle. Eventually, this brittleness caused some field problems and a vehicle recall!

Robotics

I believe that history will record that the robotic revolution, not the computer revolution as a defining point in history. Robots are really the pinnacles of the scientific, information, engineering, and computer research. Robots are a combination of many streams of technology, and thus there development has been bumpy. Robotic research and development is expensive based on the need for many disciplines. Only a handful of American universities and companies are capable of making the investment. Stanford leads in robotic software, Carnegie-Mellon in appliance type robotics, and MIT in human/robotic interfaces. Most funding is government and defense based because of the cost in this country. Japan as a nation leads in robotic development and Honda as a company. Repetitive work is fast becoming the work of robots. Paint and welding operations, in particular, have been converted to robots.

The frontier of robotic research is in humanoid type applications and flexible manufacturing operations. The push is for self-learning machines versus software and programming. Still these machines appear decades away. Appliance type robots are starting to move into the mainstream, and this is a necessary step for the field of robotics. Things like pilotless planes and service type robots are appearing. Robotic grass cutting, harvesting, and vehicle transportation are now in a commercial phase. Operations managers need to aggressively promote the application of robotics. Initial and small steps are very important. The evolution of the assembly line came in steps of a twenty year period by a determined corporate vision. The mechanical wonder of the assembly line was more a tribute to the operations managers than the engineers. Today we need both visionary management as well as engineers to bring the robotic revolution.

An Interview with Charles Sorensen

Charles Emil Sorensen (1882-1968) was a production genius and a loyal lieutenant of Henry Ford. Sorensen was the mastermind behind the Ford assembly line at Ford's Highland Park plant. He also designed the layout of Ford's mammoth Rouge Plant. His crowning achievement was the design of the Ford B-24 "Liberator" bomber plant at Willow Run during World War Two. Rising from a foundry pattern make, he became Ford's right hand man. He became known as "Cast-Iron Charlie" because of his foundry expertise. He helped the Russians build an assembly line auto industry in the 1920s. He applied materials handling systems that improved production throughout Ford Motor. He also invented steels and many product improvements. He is often remembered as the father of the V-8 engine. Magarac interviewed him at the Detroit Yacht Club where he once served as commodore.

Magarac: Many believe that you were the inventor of the Ford assembly line. How do you see it?

Sorensen: That claim got me in a lot of trouble at the end of my career, but it is the truth. "Mr. Ford said that the conveyor-assembly idea occurred to him after watching the reverse process in packing houses, where hogs and steers were braced up by hind legs on an overheard conveyor and disassembled." This is a rationalization long after the event. Mr. Ford had nothing to do with originating, planning, and carrying out the assembly line. He encouraged the work, his vision to try unorthodox methods was an example to us; and in that there is glory enough for all.[32]

Magarac: How did this revolutionary breakthrough come about?

Sorensen: It really was more evolutionary. "The essential tools and the final assembly line with its many integrated feeders resulted from an organization which continually used experimenting and improvising to get better production."

---

[32] Charles Sorenson, *My Forty Years with Ford,* (Detroit: Wayne State University Press, 2006), 129

One key advance was when I first used a conveyer system to bring radiators to the main line. Before that radiators were moved by hand and muscle from the docks to the line. At first Henry Ford hesitated at my process improvement until I showed him the calculations of the saving. Conveyors started to be used for other parts and subassemblies. My assistant superintendent Clarence Avery achieved another key advance. I had trained Avery over eight months by putting him on every job in the operation. The experience allowed him to " work out the timing schedules necessary before installation of conveyor assembly systems to motors, fenders, magnetos, and transmissions." We were able to cut manufacturing cost by 50% over a two-year period by implementing these types of improvements.

Magarac: Your success makes you the ideal person to talk to about "lean manufacture."

Sorensen: I really like the term lean manufacturing. We tried to cut the fat in all areas including inventory, handling, purchasing, material movement, scheduling, timing, and delivery times. The savings were huge in many areas. I see today, you have a focus on inventory, cycle time, tool change-over, and delivery. These areas were fundamental to our approach as well. But, as you have found, the real goal of lean manufacture is the quickest and most efficient delivery of product from conception to the hands of the customer. Our main metrics, like yours today, were cost and time based.

Magarac: How and where did you start to implement lean manufacturing?

Sorenson: It really began with the inefficiencies of our first plant at Piquette Avenue. Piquette Avenue was bigger than the Mack Avenue plant we left in 1904, but little thought other than size was put into the layout. There were several buildings requiring a lot of material and subassembly handling. The main focus at the Piquette plant was product development, which laid the groundwork for the 1908 launch of the Model T. The layout of the process had been given almost no thought. The inherent problems were paramount when in 1907 we started to plan the Highland Park plant.

We hired an experienced industrial architect in Albert Kahn, who had designed the 1903 Packard Motor plant here in Detroit. "Overall, the building's design relied on logic: raw materials were delivered to the top floor, as they were forged and machined in to finished parts made their way down the floors through more than a thousand openings Ford and Kahn had incorporated for chutes, conveyors, and tubes."[33] The plant was designed to efficiently take in and distribute boxcars of supplied parts. We opened the plant in 1910, but it remained in a state of development and expansion for many years. This was done on purpose as part of a continuous improvement plan.

Magarac: Highland Park was designed for the assembly line?

Sorensen: Not exactly. Experimentation and development work was going on concurrently at Piquette as Highland Park was being developed. In mid-1908, I was experimenting with my foreman Charlie Lewis on putting parts on a chassis being pulled by a rope. "It was then that the idea occurred to me that assembly would be easier, simpler, and faster if we moved the chassis along, beginning at one end of the plant with a frame and adding the axles and the wheels; then moving it past the stockroom, instead of moving the stockroom to the chassis."[34] The experiments were endless that summer, but I believe by August, Lewis and I had manufactured the first car by assembly line. It is the same approach, you advocate in lean manufacturing. It really encompasses the movements of Design of Experiments, Six-

---

[33] Douglas Brinkley, *Wheels for the World,* (New York: Viking, 2003), 138
[34] Sorensen, 117

Sigma, and lean manufacturing of recent years. Industrial experimentation was the heart of our approach. Our focus was the quest to reduce cycle time, and that affected all areas of the business. By 1912, our suppliers could not keep up with the manufacturing requirements, so we had to look at better supplier management. It also leads to horizontal expansion and subassembly manufacture. I would say that the Rouge Plant was the first built for the assembly line.

Magarac: Doesn't the idea of lean manufacture lend itself to spinning off subassembly production?

Sorensen: We believed supply was critical to successful assembly line operation. Time and time again, the assembly at Highland Park slowed or stopped for lack of parts. In addition, the demand we generated drove prices up. These problems led us to manufacture more parts and assemblies. This even continued at the world's most integrated auto plant at the Rouge. Take plate glass for example, in the 1920s we were buying it at 50 cents a square foot. Our demand took the price to $1.50 a square foot; even worse, the supply was not consistent. We purchased our supplier's old Pennsylvania plant, and quickly identified the inefficiencies. We then decided to build a modern facility at the Rouge Plant. We revolutionized the process making it continuous from silica sand to plate glass. We got the cost down to 20 cents a square foot. To eliminate the transportation costs of silica sand, we built a plant in Minnesota that was really continuous, and the cost dropped to 10 cents a square foot. You have to chase supply costs and delivery with the same passion as your own process.

We had the same success with steel manufacturing. Steel handling and transportation were particularly costly to our operation, but we might have lived with that if the steel mills could deliver consistently. The steel coil production cycle from raw materials to our stamping machines was twenty-one days. When we opened our steel plant at the

Rouge, we brought the cycle down to fourteen days. After a few more months of experimentation, we reached a four-day cycle. Charles Schwab, President of Bethlehem Steel, wanted to buy the plant because it was the world's best. The price came down because we could more efficiently recycle our scrap.

Magarac: Why are companies moving in the opposite direction today?

Sorensen: Global cheap labor makes it more cost effective to buy subassemblies from places like China. Many companies still have delivery problems with the long delivery lines. We gained efficiency through lean techniques, not cheap labor. I stood with Henry Ford on higher wages. We got a productivity boom with the $5 a day wage. It was a bit short lived, but it helped the workers buy more cars.

Magarac: You had economic impact that few had to make wage increases work that way.

Sorenson: Not really. I don't believe that wages were the problem. Our lean manufacturing approach could overcome the cost of higher wages. In the 1920s, our rapid manufacturing pushed the ability of the railroads to deliver on time, yet our demand allowed them to increase prices. We bought the worn-to-the- flanges Detroit, Toledo & Ironton Railroad and made it a 320 mile world-class railroad. We knew nothing of railroading, but applied our lean manufacturing principles. We ended irregular and bottlenecked delivery to suppliers and ourselves. We even improved delivery to our dealers with the technique of piggybacking new autos on freight cars. We did all this while increasing wages. Engineers got $100 more a month than other railroads. Even the trackwalkers got $300 more a year for less time. Wages would have gone even higher with a profit-sharing plan that was blocked by the government.

When the government stopped Henry from lowering freight rates, he sold it for 250% profit.

Magarac: Do you really think you could compete with Chinese and Japanese companies today?

Sorensen: I believe we could, but it would be difficult. You have to neutralize their advantages of cheap raw materials, government support, and cheap wages and benefits. Your transplant auto plants are extremely competitive because of the reduced benefits and profit-based wages. They also are highly automated with robotics. Labor and management are open to change and improvement. I believe these plants say it can be done. The question is whether Ford and General Motors can adapt, change, and retool fast enough. Certainly, the employee buyouts will help, assuming they avoid the sins of the past.

At NUMMI, a joint venture of Toyota and General Motors, lean manufacture was introduced. Workers put in 57 seconds of labor every minute, compared to 45 seconds per minute when General Motors ran the plant.[35] That's a 25% increase in efficiency. This occurred at lower wages then previously earned at General Motors. Efficiency is part of the answer, but we need a national policy to focus the nation's manufacturing mission.

Magarac: Isn't lean manufacturing a Japanese contribution?

Sorensen: Again, I believe their contribution is overstated. They did teach us about quick tool change. Toyota, after World War II, faced a much different problem than we did at Highland Park or the Rouge Plant. Toyota didn't have the luxury of massive runs of a single product. We had assembly lines dedicated to single models. Toyota had to produce several different models and product on the same line each

---

[35] T.A. Kochan, R. D. Lansbury, and J. MacDuffle, eds., *After Lean Production*, (Ithaca: Cornell University Press, 1997)

week. Our tooling was highly specialized and long term; theirs' was flexible and capable of quick change out. They measured die changes in minutes while we measured it in days. It was a path we never foresaw a need for. Now quick tooling change is at the heart of mass customization. The good news is that our inefficiencies of the past are like money in the bank.

Magarac: What do you mean?

Sorensen: I believe you call it low hanging fruit! Let me relate a recent example I heard from a consultant friend of mine. Many stamping plants and die shops can relate to this. This particular plant was a blanking plant with a product mix of hundreds of blank products. The die storage for the blank sizes and products was in a building two blocks away. My friend was asked to help implement lean manufacture, but his pay would be based on hard results. He was amazed at how easy the savings were to find. A die change would average eight to ten hours. The die sequence is common to many American organizations, which were never under the cost pressures of the global market.

First, once production planning called for a product change, two general purpose workers would be assigned to drive the truck to the die warehouse and get the correct die for the new product run. Often these workers were in the middle of other projects, and/or the truck was tied up. Once these workers got the truck and arrived at the warehouse, some additional problems arose. The dies were often not clearly marked nor were the computer inventory positions updated. The search for the correct die commonly took over an hour. Finally, the die would arrive at the blanking operation after as much as a three-hour wait. The blank shop foreman would be called to get the die to the proper machine, and to get some maintenance people to put the die in. The biggest hangup here was that dies arrived with rust and dirt, requiring hours of cleaning. After cleaning, the actual installation was delayed by lack of proper tools.

My friend was able to clean almost five hours out of the operation with little effort. First, he established an identification and inventory retrieval, which was based on tags and clear die marking. Simple but powerful. A priority labor assignment system was established to have workers and the truck available for potential die change. Again, nothing amazing, just improved communication and a more systematic approach. Finally, the biggest improvement was to improve storage of dies with humidity warehouse control and roof repair. Dies were also oiled and covered, thus they arrived clean and ready, saving hours of cleaning. This is the type of savings that is available because of loss of the competitive edge over the years. Ten years ago, this company had no foreign competition; now it has lost half its market to foreign competition.

Magarac: Engineers have pointed out this is part of the entropic deterioration of American industry.

Sorensen: I'm not an engineer, but I think I understand what you mean. We got a bit lazy. Systems became sloppy and non-responsive. As an industry, we stretched the life of our equipment, allowed a loose work ethic to evolve, and lost our sense of competition. The global market put us in competition with lean, hungry, and sacrificing foreign manufacturers. Global competitors have the best equipment and technology as well. I think, we found these types of built-in inefficiencies as we bought steel mills, glass houses, and railroads in the 1920s. People marveled at our success without any specific industry knowledge. We applied simple solutions to inefficiencies that were built into these plants over the years. They were clear to us as outsiders, but almost invisible to those who worked there. This is the real strength of lean manufacture; it is a matter of hidden costs. It's like mining gold. I would love to be a consultant today.

Magarac: Do you think our problems are cultural?

Sorensen: Not really. I believe there is a lack of leadership in industry and government. I helped put Ford plants around the world, and capitalist systems like ours actually have an inherent ability to innovate. I saw leadership as the difference. God knows, I had my problems with Henry Ford, and we clearly credit him with too many innovations. Still, Henry Ford's vision of a car for the masses drove innovation and improvement. Ford was a leader; you can't take that away from him. He forced you to make improvements. He demanded it on a daily basis. Henry did have the advantage of building his own organization, so we were not fighting old ideas. When we took over companies and plants, we stripped the old organization out. The biggest fight for innovation can be the old organization, so I guess you can say culture has a type of impact.

Magarac: Don't you need to keep the people who know the operation when you take over a plant?

Sorensen: Why? Many times these were the people that caused the problem. Non-operating types on Wall Street worry about that. Many times you need to strip management that is disruptive. Keep the workers- that is the necessary experience base. Bring in new leadership, make changes, all while listening to the workforce. Often, the workers are well aware of the old management's mistakes, and can become vital to necessary change.

Magarac: What about the Union? Isn't the old union leadership part of the problem too?

Sorensen: When I started as a pattern maker I joined the union, but never had any passion for it. When I started at Ford, some pattern makers tried to get me to form a union, but I turned away. I had mixed feelings about the union throughout my career, but today I see a further danger in their resistance to change. Wages and benefits have to be looked at in new ways, and that is a sensitive issue with union leaders. Work rules and job classifications needed to be reviewed as to their role. The radical change needed is extremely difficult for the union leadership. I can't blame them, in a way. It's the type of change that requires sacrifice. I certainly wouldn't want to be a union leader today. In fact, I avoided labor negotiations in my day. I prefer to chase process improvements, yet you are correct that the union has a major role. The whole system needs to be lean. There can be no sacred cows that are excluded from the quest that includes management pay systems and benefits. Union leaders need to educate the workers on the issue, it's always tough to reduce pay and benefits.

Magarac: Lean manufacturing is really greenfield thinking?

Sorensen: I assume you mean by Greenfield starting to review the system as if you are starting at the new plant site. Yes, that has to be done. If you started from scratch how would manage it, lay it out, what would you pay, even who would you supply? Everything needs to be reconsidered.

Magarac: Even customers?

Sorensen: Customers are part of the system. Many auto suppliers have gone bankrupt supplying customers, such as Ford and General Motors. I would re-evaluate customers. Do you have the process capability to meet the specifications demanded by the customer? Trying to supply a customer without process capability is economic suicide, but it is occurring every day. Who wants to turn down a big order? But that is exactly what you have to do many times.

Identifying and calculating your process capability is fundamental to a lean manufacturing program. Process capability is the key metric for a plant, product, or piece of equipment. It compares statistically to what you are producing to the specifications demanded by the customer. Process capability has to be known and understood by all, in particular, sales people and upper management, who have a tendency to take business with the idea that operations can achieve a manufacturing miracle? Once you have collected the data and calculated your process capability, then you can make decisions such as the amount of inspection needed or whether new equipment is needed, but you could also choose not to supply. Aggressive order taking can lead to excessive quality and reject costs to an organization.

Chapter Eight

The Structure of the
Global Organization

A causal reading of the business pages might suggest that the global organization is lean and mean. Middle management and hierarchical layers, one would think are the enemy of the globalization, but hierarchical organization is not the issue. It's efficiency and productivity that defines the nature of global organizations, not body counts. Global organizations are leaner because they are efficient, but global organizations tend to evolve along the traditional view of management span of control. The laws of capitalism in the global organization define wages and labor costs. Socialism is a luxury that global organizations cannot afford. The global organization is not foreign to America, but a reflection of the American corporation prior to the depression of the 1930s. It's a corporation built on self-reliance. Certainly, it's a fearful picture for today's American, but we can move to (or more properly back to) this paradigm. First, we to face the type of organization needs that succeed in the global marketplace.

The global organization exists for the simple goal of supplying a competitive product or service. Its community service is ancillary in that it supplies jobs and tax dollars. Wages, benefits, prices, quality, and salaries are based on the global market place. The global organization assumes a global free market, which in reality is rarely the case. It also assumes a consumer driven market as envisioned by Adam Smith. Thus if a government chooses to subsidize its companies, national labor in another country may suffer, but the consumer always wins. In today's politics, the consumer is king. Neither American political party has shown much interest in returning to the protective tariffs of McKinley Republicanism. Thus the first law of today's globalization is the consumer always wins even at the expense of manufacturing jobs, good benefits, and high wages. The first step to succeeding in a globalized market is to accept the reality of the global market place, and for most of us, that's a tough step. It's easier to complain about unfair competition, the Chinese, or the Mexicans. I was one of them in my steel career, but I came to realize the government was not going to help the steel industry. The politicians were common at the factory gates in an election year, but scarce when tariffs came up in Congress.

The bottom line for the business organization is let someone else fight the battle or join forces with the workers and unions. Political alliances are necessary, but the organization cannot plan on seeing any help. Corporate alliances make better sense in the long run. Mergers to built size are not necessarily the answer. In the 1980s, the US steel industry merged to gain efficiencies that weren't there. They only produced a bigger pile of costs and inefficiencies. Transnational mergers, on the other hand, have proved more successful. A global structure allows the organization to play the competitive factors. In steel these were tough to find. The Japanese were willing to form joint ventures with American companies to develop market inroads, but wanted no part of American steel's structural costs. The Japanese had extensive alliances and ventures with LTV Steel, but did not jump into saving LTV from bankruptcy. The Japanese realized LTV's health, pension and wage structure required a major changes. The same was true of the Bethlehem Steel and National Steel collapse. History would suggest that a Ford-General Motors merger could not change the inefficiencies, only compound them.

Vision defines structure

Globalization greatest blow to American manufacturing was a loss of vision and role. It of course starts at a national level. In the 1830s, the Whig Party and the ultimately the Republican changed the national vision from an agrarian utopia to a manufacturing empire. At present, we have no real national vision as to our national role, which to a degree limits even business to develop their own vision. The government, however, is not the creator of vision, it is the population. Manufacturing and business need to set the direction, not government. It is therefore a business manager's responsibility to set vision for the company's role in a global market. It was the vision of early manufacturing mangers that revolutionized the agrarian vision of our nation. The struggle of globalization has left American business unsure of its role, but even more so we lack business leaders, industrialists, and capitalists that can lead.

Middle Management is a Natural

One effect of globalization on American firms has been downsizing, and with that has come the elimination of middle management. It has been seen as a fast way to cut salaries and payroll. The theme of "lean and mean" has been heralded as the mantra of globalization. The result has been a destruction of traditional organizational structure. Clearly, organizations need to be lean, but they need to be efficient too. American companies are not going to gain advantage in the global market by job cutting and payroll reductions. The wage advantage belongs to China and Asia. We need lean organizations that can increase productivity. We must have an organization that can win the productivity and profitability war.

In western history, hierarchical structure is a natural organizational process. We have seen churches, monasteries, governments, armies, clubs, committees, and factories all naturally grow into hierarchical organizations over the centuries. In my own consulting of small machining and manufacturing operations, I see many small companies adopt a multilevel approach. This is true also in the small company service business. Take Bonfe's Auto Service and Body Repair in St. Paul. Bonfe's is a 26-employee shop with a multilevel approach. Management consists of the owner, general managers, and production managers. The production managers oversee the work in process of the three main departments of the repair business – collision, mechanical, and detail services. The general managers handle the mechanical segment and the body shop (collision). The set up is a mirror image of that of the fourteenth century Arsenal of Venice! The functional differences of the units require a middle manager to optimize productivity.

The multilevel approach allows each focus on the specific marketing, training, and unique operating needs such as insurance management in the collision business. More importantly, these middle managers have made Bonfe a leader in the application of technology. The company has six common computer systems. The collision segment has a shop management system and two electronic estimating programs. The repair side has a shop management system, customer database system, and estimating. Computerized alignment, paint mixing, and MIG welding augment this. This technology gives Bonfe a real edge in service. The development of these systems would have been lacking without middle management. The front line production managers didn't have the time or expertise to implement and integrate these systems.

Middle managers owe their very existence to organizational structure. Again, middle managers are the product of the very organization they manage. Also, the ability of the middle manager to achieve organizational goals is dependent on the organization itself. This interdependence on the organization makes the manning of, design of, and planning for the organization the first priority of the middle manager. The middle manager must, by necessity, leave an imprint on the organization. The middle manager has three functions to perform in relationship to organizations – (1) job design, (2) organizational connectivity, and (3) manning.

Job design puts the middle manager into the role of artist. Job design requires breathing life into a corporate vision. The middle manager is at the point where vision and reality as well as mission and structure meet. The middle manager must develop a job where top management's vision meets the lower manager's reality. Without middle management, this welding of vision to reality will never occur. To leave this critical function in flat organizations to lower or upper management is to miss an opportunity to forge the link to maximize productivity. In addition, it is necessary in taller organizations that middle managers have the autonomy to perfect the function of job design.

Job design sounds bureaucratic and it is. Bureaucracy is a lost type of organization, yet is naturally favored by many employees. Over the last ten years, I have tested university business students on their bureaucratic tendencies versus free style organization preferences. Overwhelmingly, these young risk-taking students in a decade of economic boom favor the attributes of stability, clear job definition, and hierarchical career progression. At first, it was surprising to me, but in follow-up decisions, I found the social scars of downsizing in their families, friends, and cultural experiences. Bureaucratic design requires middle management guidance. Too many times the middle manager is asked to implement a job and manage it without being part of the design. The disappearance of the middle manager's role of design is part of the lost grail. The middle manager must function as an integral link in the organizational hierarchy.

The purpose of that link is organizational connectivity. The middle manager takes the idealism and vision of top management and merges it with the realism of front line supervision. Many times top management sets multiple objectives such as 100% on time delivery and zero defects. Both objectives are admirable and idealistic, but on the back shift, the rubber meets the road. For example, a foreman has a shipment ready to go; in fact, it must go to be on time at General Motors. The problem is there is some doubt about the quality. The well-conceived corporate objectives now create an ambiguity at the lower level. A decision must be made and possibly one of the objectives compromised. There exist no directions, only two seemly contrasting objectives. It is at this point of changing entropy and ambiguity that the middle manager interprets the organizational needs and goals in light of individual needs. Without this link, idealism and realism cannot be bridged in the organization. This role of pontiff (*bridge-builder*) is fundamental to the organization.

From my own experience, the role of pontiff is the very essence of organizational connectivity. While this function is usually informal, it flows directly from organizational authority. It is the role of the old industrial "boss" so admired in basic industries and part of the American legend. However, to assure organizational connectivity, manning is critical.

Manning requirements flow from job design and reinforce connectivity. Middle managers need to have complete authority and freedom to man the organizations. Organizations should not be the result of political compromises, downsizing, or centralized personnel decisions. In the last few decades, such organizational manning practices eroded the middle manager's very ability to manage and the organization's ability to achieve goals. Organizations need to reflect the middle manager. Technical qualifications are the least important in manning decisions. Factors such as attitude, people skills, etc. are paramount. In the end, the middle manager must feel the potential employee fits this image. Too many people are hired based on individual accomplishments versus their potential to be a loyal organizational soldier.

With job design, proper manning and organizational connectivity, the middle manager has the keys to organizational success. More importantly, it is a set of keys unique to the middle manager.

Training managers

Management training is the biggest problem. Our college-educated managers are trained to be CEOs and executives. The majority of them will start at lower level management positions, which they have no training for. Textbook case studies are written for the student to role model as a CEO of the company. They graduate with the ability to make executive decisions, but have no idea of the nature of the lower level decisions, they will be making. The lower and middle manager will rarely have the flexibility of a CEO in their ability to implement change, yet that is what they had in their case studies. Their training tends also to make them critical of upper management before they have the understanding of the organization.

An Interview with William Brown Dickson

William Brown Dickson (1866-1942) became known as Carnegie Steel's conscience. Coming from a middle class family, he still started as a laborer in the steel mills in the boroughs of Pittsburgh. He was only a boy, working as a clerk during the Homestead Strike of 1892, when Charles Schwab selected him to be part of his management team. Ultimately, he would rise to Vice-president of United States Steel in1911. He was often a lone executive fighting for better hours, the elimination of Sunday work, better working conditions, and employee benefits. In 1915, he with several ex-Carnegie executives, formed a new experimental steel company (Midvale Steel). At Midvale, he experimented with employee ownership, and what became known as "Industrial Democracy." The experiment failed because of pressures from other capitalists such as J. P. Morgan. Eventually, his friend Charles Schwab, then at Bethlehem Steel, saved Midvale from bankruptcy by bringing it into Bethlehem Steel. Schwab arranged for a good retirement for Dickson, but removed him from active management. Dickson moved into consulting and politics during the 1930s depression. Magarac met him at the Homestead Strike Memorial.

Magarac: Great to finally meet you. My dad was a great admirer of yours. I have heard that it was the experience at Homestead that changed you forever.

Dickson: I watched the battle evolve form my home in Swissvale across the river. I had worked and lived with the steelworkers, and it was upsetting to see the bloodshed. Initially, I supported the company because I was anti-union. My father had owned coal mines in Swissvale and Swisshelm Park, and had been threatened by the "Molly Maguires."[36] Still, I hated to see the working conditions of the mills and the struggles of the workers families. Homestead really began a mental quest for a better working environment. I believed that Schwab's advances in productivity could further be improved by better working conditions.

Magarac: I'm told you even disliked the living environs of Pittsburgh because of the industrial setting.

Dickson: Yes, look at the beauty of the Monongahela over there minus the great Homestead Works of my day. I had

---

[36] The "Molly Maguires" were radical union supporters in the Pennsylvania mines. They were known for secrecy and violence.

read Jules Verne's novel, *The Begum's Millions*, which contrasted a steel town like Pittsburgh and its affect on workers to one of natural beauty. Verne clearly showed the difference between a technological dystopia and a workingman's utopia. Verne, of course, was promoting the success of Robert Owen in Scotland. I was also a supporter of George Westinghouse in seeing the link between environment and productivity. I myself moved the family out of Pittsburgh to the beauty of Montclair, New Jersey.

Magarac: Yet your effort to change the environment and work conditions was attacked by the union and your own management in 1918 at Midvale Steel. Your plan for representation of the workingmen at Midvale was considered by many as a substitute for the union.

Dickson: "No, I was perfectly willing to allow the union to represent the men, if the union could run it to the advantage of the men in the shop and in fairness to the company. My doctrine is not narrow. I am out for the general welfare- the greatest good to the greatest number and a square deal for all."[37] The plan was ahead of its time. I called it "Industrial Democracy," and it was similar to a proposal of John Rockefeller at his Colorado steel plant. The times called for a new approach.

Magarac: Tell me a little more about the plan?

Dickson: First, I hoped to use employee/management committees to handle the actual running of the company. The beauty of this approach was to free managers, who were "spending 50% of their time on annoyances." Under the plan, the company and employees would jointly contribute to a fund to cover sickness, insurance, and retirement benefits. The plan included stock ownership and profit sharing.

---

[37] A Dickson quote to National Labor Board, 1919; Gerald Eggert, *Steelmasters and Labor Reform, 1886-1923,* (Pittsburgh: University of Pittsburgh Press, 1981), 121

"During the first nine months of operation at the Johnstown plant, for example, the plan adjusted hundreds of disputes over working conditions and wages, some of many years' standing. Toilets, lavatories, and baths were installed for the convenience of the workers. A home building loan program, financed by the company, was instituted at the request of the employees' representatives. Baseball and football teams were started, and the company opened a free bathing beach to employees and townspeople. Even the company reservoirs were opened for employee fishing. The mere existence of grievance machinery seemed to reduce instances of abuse by foremen and department superintendents and to give workers some sense that they would be fairly treated."

Magarac: What is applicable today when the issue is not so much abuse, but overburdening of all by benefits in a global market?

Dickson: I agree that things are a lot different, but there are also similarities. I believed in ownership in the company, but that also brings responsibility. Employees and the owners have to work together. I testified often before Congress on the lack of pensions in this country. Pensions are important to basic productivity. Maslow clearly demonstrated that basic security needs must be satisfied before you can motivate people with achievement goals and rewards. I am a strong believer that the company needs to address pensions, but it must be a mutual program. This is critical. Your 401K plans are the type of thing I was proposing in the 1920s. The government IRA accounts are another plus.

Magarac: But few employees are putting money into 401Ks and IRAs?

Dickson: Even in my day this was a problem, but it was then more related to low wages. Low wages is not the problem today. Employees need financial education as to how these work and why they need to save. This should be the role of the company. Like you, however, I am amazed how few people save for their future. This generation is used to the corporate and government benefits of a previous time of America's economic dominance. The panics, recessions, and depressions of my time hardened us and prepared us.

Magarac: I agree that today there is a view of the wealthy company.

Dickson: It was no different in my day. "The worker needs to know more about the actual problems of management. They need to learn something about overhead, about marketing difficulties, about the dependence of production and production conditions upon marketing and the dependence of marketing upon economic production, about the numberless hazards and chances of loss, which their employer must face. They need, in short, more of the manager's point of view. And the obvious way to give it to them is to let them have some part in handling management problems."[38] The type of understanding required calls for a deep trust and that is why I had employee representatives at all meetings, including the Board of Directors. Every single meeting must have an employee representative present. Every decision must be made in the presence of an employee representative. There can be no secrets. It must be open, accepting the problems and misunderstandings that might initially occur. In good times, expect calls for more wage increases, but hopefully the trust gained will allow understanding of the need to reduce benefits. Trust will take time, but honesty is absolutely essential. One lie, one hidden set of books, or faked document, and all is lost.

Magarac: Most feel today that companies are wealthy and can afford higher wages?

---

[38] *System Magazine,* June 1919

Dickson: "The typical workman now has only the haziest ideas as to the nature and function of the business he is in. Often he thinks of the resources as a kind of inexhaustible reservoir, from which the employer can raise wages as much as he likes by simply opening the spigot wider. Look into almost any workman's thought on the subject, and you will find something like that. Small wonder the demands of labor are often unreasonable."

Magarac: But labor and management don't trust each other, which seems to make it hopeless.

Dickson: I had anti-union views because I feared this might happen. Management got a union because of its abuses, and now you have another element in the mix. The union has its own motives. It's a difficult situation but the worker must be put first. All three groups have the common goal of survival. Unfortunately, labor relations is the slowest process in a business. It is years behind what is happening in the marketplace because of the lack of trust and additional infrastructure. The needed changes are too small and coming too late. To retake the competitive world edge will require a daring and major change by all. In the last twenty years, you have seen the steel industry and United Steelworkers fail to cut deep enough. The result is a mall there instead the great Homestead mill. Globalization takes companies into cutthroat competition, small steps will fail.

Magarac: The situation is difficult with health benefits. You fought for health benefits as well as pensions. What do you suggest?

Dickson: The solution probably requires a bigger brain than mine, but I have a few ideas. The companies are in a very difficult position. The government is allowing "free" competition with foreign companies that pay no benefits as well as low wages. If the government will not tariff this competition to make things fair, then the government must assume responsibility for the workers' health care. This was a basic principle of the McKinley tariff of my day. This type of "free" trade lowers prices for the consumer while stripping them of health care and pensions. Unfortunately, it appears the government is not interested in addressing this problem. The burden then falls to the company and the worker. The company should set up mutual health accounts for the worker. These accounts have favorable tax consideration. I like the shared responsibility, which is needed to help control health costs. Co-pays on prescription have helped reduce costs. Some companies are returning to having a company doctor to reduce costs. Usually, these are retired doctors who visit twice a week. I like the formation of pools of smaller companies. I think the unions will have to get personally involved in the management of healthcare. This is not a company problem; it is a national problem.

Magarac: I assume you feel the same about disability and pensions?

Dickson: No. Disability insurance is a company responsibility; it is the cost of doing business. Furthermore, I believe safety has to be given corporate priority, and that is why the expense and responsibility for disability and injury insurance must be corporate. "The cost of industrial accidents should be made a part of the cost of production and that the men injured and the families of men killed or injured should be given compensation or relief irrespective of employer negligence." Of course, the problem you have today is outrageous lawsuits at every turn. We need a government-imposed truce on this type of warfare from both sides. In 1906, I formed the first safety department at a major company- United States Steel. I believe disability and injury insurance should be overly generous, but employees should also be restricted on lawsuits that can hurt the company and threaten jobs. I believe that if some reason is restored, then disability insurance could be a plus for all.

The real issue here is safety. Safety has to be fundamental to the operation, not an ancillary function. I believe government has a role in safety. OSHA is one of those government programs, I have praised. More cooperation is needed to improve safety and assure financial help to those injured. One of the best company programs at Carnegie Steel tapped into the competitive spirit that had been fostered by the company. We had interdepartmental safety contests with cash rewards. We were able to cut our serious accidents by 43% over a four-year period.[39] I also agree with the findings of Fredrick Taylor in his report to Congress that the most productive companies are also the safest.

Magarac: What about pensions then?

Dickson: Pensions are mutual responsibility, as I have said.

Magarac: What about profit sharing and ownership?

Dickson: The employees, union, and management must all have ownership. Profitsharing is a start, but it lacks the feel many times of ownership. The type of profitsharing Andrew Carnegie gave his managers was real ownership. In this program, pay was made up of wages and stock. Several hard-headed Irish managers, like Bill Jones, wanted dollars, not stock, but those who participated became wealthy. I understand the independence of Jones, who given the money would take care of his own benefits. I believe stock should be part of the wage; however, because it brings the employee into the business- both ups and downs. The union should also be invested in the company. I realize this represents a new paradigm, but globalization requires this change. Ownership must involve the rewards and risks. Today, we see demands for ownership with the risk liability of doing business. I

---

[39] Dickson address to the American Iron & Steel Institute, October 14, 1910

don't see profit-sharing as an employee benefit; I see it as a business requirement.

But ownership is more than stock ownership. It must involve an active role of employees in the business. Many employee-owned companies have failed because employees never really felt like owners. Employees need to sit in on all operational meetings. Their say has to have impact. Maybe more importantly, it builds trust in the long run. We have to move beyond "quality circles" and "Improvement Teams" to real day-to-day involvement in the real infrastructure. A lot of these teams are "feel good" programs outside the real infrastructure of the company. They are opposed by the union and front line managers alike. In my day, top management opposed real representation as you do today. It's a difficult subject, but we need to do things differently.

Magarac: You advised discussing all wage cuts with the people prior to any action, but had little support among your own managers. How would you suggest taking such actions today?

Dickson: First and foremost, all decisions, including wages, must be done with employee representatives present. This is part of the trust I've been talking about. Wage reductions are problematic because they usually result in a corresponding reduction in productivity. Carnegie was once convinced that there should be a sliding scale. Wages would rise and fall with prices. It was our plant manager at Braddock, Bill Jones, who resisted this approach based on its impact on productivity. We were even more sensitive in our day because wages made up 85 percent of the cost of labor. I lost this battle with my management at Midvale, and they unilaterally reduced wages. That action destroyed our experiment in industrial democracy. It gave rise to a union, and the ultimate failure of Midvale Steel. If wage decisions are excluded then you cannot be truly employee driven. I still believe the possibility of wage cuts can be discussed if there is trust. A number of options can be considered, such as less vacation, a few donated hours, or special saving accounts for better times. Many times workers will accept a wage cut to save jobs. Frankly, I realize that capital and labor must fully share the rewards and losses, but I could not get capital to share the rewards, nor could I get labor to share the risks. I still strongly believe that present union-management structure, only reinforces that inability on both sides.

Magarac: Do you believe the automotive worker buyouts will work?

Dickson: I certainly pray they do. I believe the company and the union are acting responsibly with the buyouts. The buyouts help reduce pension, health, and wage costs in the long run. Delphi is replacing many of the buyouts with temporary labor at $14 an hour versus $28 an hour. The company realizes, like Bill Jones did that you cannot reduce wages of the present workers without a reduction in productivity. Captain Bill had it right almost a hundred years before management scientists developed the theory to support it. You know it today as the Equity Theory of Work Motivation.[40] For Captain Bill, it was common sense, reduce wages and the workers will adjust their output. This buyout approach allows older workers to continue at the old wage rate, while bringing new employees at a new scale. The use of temporary labor is also important because it allows the company to adjust to market conditions, which would have made Carnegie happy. Temporary labor is the type of buffer needed in a global market. It really is a beautiful solution to a very difficult issue, and both sides worked it out. My only concern is if it will be drastic enough. The steel industry tried buyout packages in the 1980s, but still could not reach foreign labor costs. What is required is lower cost and more flexible labor to replace the workers moved out.

---

[40] P. Goodman and A. Friedman, "An Examination of Adams' Theory of Inequity," *Administrative Science Quarterly,* September 1971

Magarac: But the steel industry never got the approval to replace with temporary labor or some form of cheaper labor?

Dickson: True. I think the automotive industry is more aggressive and competitive. The package should at least make the American companies competitive with the foreign transplants. I hope the union will show flexibility on automation as well. I worked five years as a laborer in the steel mills, and it's hard to see these global adjustments needed today. We all long for the 1950s and similar decades in American history. It is a turning point, like the Homestead Strike, which should change things for the better. Of course, there will be no monument built to the impact on globalization on American labor, but the impact will be as significant.

One thing the steel industry did do right is the creation of multicrafts or supercrafts in the 1990s. Again, grandfathering was used to protect the older workers. Crafts were combined so that one supercraftsman could do the work of three or four specialized craftsmen, and do it faster. It took more training, but also created higher paying jobs. These are all examples of the cooperation I struggled for in 1919.

Magarac: Do you believe unions have a role today?

Dickson: I don't know. Unions resulted from the barbaric treatment of workers in my day. They also seemed to fit what men, like J. P. Morgan, Judge Gary, and others wanted. Unions allowed for aggressive, warlike solutions to wage issues. I think unions may well face a slow death as you are seeing. The real problem, however, is decades of lack of trust in the big unionized industries. Only ownership and trust can make a real difference in the struggle in these industries. Maybe, globalization will bring about a new generation that can look beyond the past.

Magarac: How did you feel about the great iconic managers of your day such as Carnegie?

Dickson: Of course, I was a Carnegie man, but it was Bill Jones that inspired me. Carnegie remains an enigma. I had no time for men, such as Henry Clay Frick and Homestead plant manager John Potter. Schwab was a personal friend, but we often disagreed on labor policy. In general, my labor ideas were too advanced for the time. I had a major dislike for the first owners of United States Steel, J. P. Morgan and Judge Gary. Their approach was what I called "welfare capitalism." It was paternal and autocratic in nature, but treated labor as plantation slaves. I believe this welfare capitalism set us up for the competitive failure of today. In the 1930s, I believe the American government fully adopted the system of welfare capitalism as a defense against socialism. Such a system can thrive in periods of economic dominance, but fails with international competition.

Magarac: Your record seems to have one inconsistency from my point of view. In the 1930s you worked against the anti-trust laws, but wanted tariff reductions.

Dickson: The inconsistency can be explained by my "free market" or anti-government approach. I tried to put together a political mix of consumers, laborers, and producers. The anti-tariff plank was more of a global one because tariff wars appeared to have brought on the depression. I also felt that American industries could reduce inefficiencies through consolidation. I guess, it was one of the few points I agreed with J. P. Morgan on. I eventually moderated my view on tariff reductions after people like your father pressured me.

Chapter Nine

Playing by the Rules

The Career Pinnacle

It was the day I had dreamed of – a career achievement. New York – New York was playing on the radio and that is how I felt. I left a small town steel company to be quality manager at a major steel plant in the city of steel. That day, after a year wait, the promotion had come at Jones and Laughlin Steel Pittsburgh Works. (Jones and Laughlin was then part of the now defunct LTV Steel.) I had patiently worked under a detailed-oriented boss and a great upper management team. My boss had been promoted so the transfer of power was presidential. He showed me forms, techniques, and procedures. Finally he appeared a bit nervous and said there was a file he kept locked he needed to show me. The file had gone back many years and had similarly been passed on to him. I knew this was not good news.

So here was the bad news for the day. The file was a thirty-year record of "changed" steel chemistries. Steel is made to a set of chemistry specifications demanded by national standards or contractual customer requirements. Large batches of steel (50 to 200 tons) are produced to these chemistries that can cover specifications on up to 20 various individual elements. Not meeting an individual requirement can cause the whole heat of steel to be scrapped at significant cost to the company. More commonly, the last is measured in the additional production time needed to "work" the steel into specifications. In most cases, the steelmakers can meet the specifications from a technical standpoint, but it costs operating time and effort. Thus, steelmakers always push the limit, and if they go over, they pressure quality control to "accept it". Generally the close calls are handled by "rounding off the numbers". Chemistries variations could cause problems in the field, and in most cases, certified lab chemistry was required from the steel mill. Bigger misses required more imagination that leads to changing the chemical records. The quality control manager had to approve this action and thus, the file, although because of the culture, I'm sure some changes occurred without even the quality manager being aware of. There were, of course, significant ethical issues here, but what was missed is that there's an even bigger productivity problem.

For sure, the plant had a problem meeting chemical specifications, not because they lacked the ability, but because they lacked clear ethical rules. In effect, they couldn't improve because they didn't play by the rules. Not playing by the rules allows for variation, sloppy work, and lack of targets. Great golfers like Arnold Palmer realize the importance of playing by rules. Most of us play golf using our own rules such as "winter rules", bad turf rules", etc. Palmer, like all the pros, understood that you couldn't improve unless you learn to live with your mistakes. Not playing by the rules fosters mediocrity in individuals as well as companies. Long run it shuts down improvement.

Let's look at a somewhat unusual application of rules to improve productivity. Mark Atteberry tells the story of a frustrated high basketball coach in his book, the *Samson Syndrome*. This coach was sick and tired of his players missing critical free throws. The coach instituted a rule that any player missing a free throw during the game would have to take ten extra laps around the gym. This is not exactly the type of rule that usually increases productivity. At first it did hurt morale among team members. As time went on the rule became another rule and was accepted as such. With this acceptance the free throw percentage went from 58 percent to 69 percent. The team began to win more games and won a tough conference game on a last second free throw. When rules are in place and there are consciences for not following them, improvement will come.

Not Playing by the Rules Assures Unprofitability

It was a tough decision but I had to leave the past where it was. Still I decided that I had to improve these questionable practices for the future. Unfortunately that improvement would come slow. I couldn't say tomorrow we meet the national standards for sulfur or the steel's scrap! I started with a tighter range and worked the range down to the national standards. I immediately applied a zero tolerance on all critical steels. Specifications engineers argued that sulfur wasn't important and such an approach would be the ruin of the financially troubled company. As I moved up the ladder with the problem I got more support. I learned that questionable ethics is not a top driven problem; in fact it is just as much middle driven and bottom driven. The top, however, is the only level that can prevent its spread. Cultural factors, however, are set by the top and infiltrate to the lowest level. In fact, the extent of the sulfur problem at LTV was really a middle lower management "secret". The lower management metallurgists and chemists had resisted ethical behavior in favor of more imposing cultural factors. I'm not trying to take away from the responsibility of the top. Yet it is necessary to realize that top management is somewhat naïve, and also they like being naïve.

Top management thinks in absolutes and has, many times, little understanding how the organization functions. The top, for example, kicks off the year with a goal of a 20% increase in on-time deliveries and improved product quality. These seem like good objectives, and yet they cause confusion as you move down the organization. Let's take, for example, a batch of steel needed by General Motors to keep a plant running. The first sample shows its high sulfur. If the steelmakers take the time to refine the sulfur down, it will make the order late. The decision to use the steel at the high sulfur level will be based on middle and lower management's perception of which objective top management values most production or quality. Prior to going to Pittsburgh Steel Works, I was on the other side of the field. A melt shop superior then, I knew well production was job one. In reality, the supervisor can't win and probably one objective will need to be sacrificed. Of course, top management likes it gray since they are free of the blame and are decision free. Also, top management can then second-guess, based on the ultimate customer response to the decision. In effect, the responsibility is pushed down the organization.

Some years ago, Gen. Taguchi (famous for industrial statistics) suggested that workers only be told the target, not the specifications. He believed that would make the worker strive to do the best each time. The concept was beyond what anyone could fathom. We are not only conditioned to work to acceptable ranges but to constantly challenge those ranges. Taguchi had touched not on a quality issue, but in reality, an ethical issue and productivity issue. Unfortunately it is an issue strongly interrelated to our cultural view. We seem to overlook the relationship between ethics and productivity. We see today that the use of "loose", "aggressive", or plain unethical accounting does more than adjust the immediate profits problem – it creates a system of unprofitability for the long term. Maybe worse, it creates a culture of unethical behavior that defies responsibility and management control.

Ethics and Entropy

The difference between crime and unethical business behavior is that crime is a relatively fast action while unethical behavior is a slow process that gets you to the same place. Ethical issues are entropic, that is, with time all organizations tend towards disorder, loosened rules, and unethical behavior. It takes leadership and discipline to reverse this entropy.

Getting back to my sulfur level experience, there was a clear upward trend. Let's say the national standard was .03 maximum for sulfur. Quality control started to approve .031, .033, and even .035 (writing them back in the record). Each previous approval became the "new standard". Without any system or management restraints, this trend will continue. Specifications continue to widen until a field or customer problem causes a review and usually tighter specifications (temporarily). Furthermore, unethical decisions will be pushed down the organization and engrained in the system and lost to management's view. In many cases, upper management is truly ignorant of the problem. That's the nature of organizational entropy.

Another effect of organizational entropy is that it retards technology improvements. Sulfur removal technology had also improved over the time period, but liberal rules made the investment "unnecessary". Sulfur removal technology might have even developed faster by the laws of economic demand but for the unethical behavior. The changing of sulfur records took away demand. This is how unethical behavior actually inhibits technology improvement as well. This is the long-term cost of short-term "profitability". It also demonstrates how unethical practices can affect the economy as a whole by preventing improvement.

Some Things Never Change

Problems of ethics in business are far from new. It is inherent to the nature of man. In the past, men, realizing this, reinforced ethics through government and moral codes.

Early civilizations in China used autocratic government to assure ethical behavior in the economic system. An early business manual, *Records of Etiquette* (400 BC), defined the production and sale of handicrafts. Strict regulating by the government of behavior and production resulted in superior quality and workmanship but brought many drawbacks. First, such pre-control of business and over-restrictive laws short-circuited natural economic systems. Costs clearly went out of control in early China. Government regulation of business ethics was inefficient and costly.The high demand on pure business behavior and quality production served the monarchic class well but hurt the common people in high prices. It was a clear lesson in the high costs of government regulation.

Closer to the roots of our society is the theocracy of ancient Israel. Israel regulated the problem with a combination of a national moral code as well as individual religion. These are documented in the bible and Talmud. Things like fair scales and weights as well as business practices are embedded in the bible. Honest measurement is highly emphasized – "Ye shall do no unrighteousness in judgment, in meter yard, in weight or in measure". (LEV 14:35) Of course in Israel, the government, moral code, and religion were unified producing some government regulation with an individual behavior focus. This blend did not interfere with the economic system by over regulating it or causing a price increase due to regulation; instead it improved market function.

This blend of individual ethics with some government regulation in early Israel produced a profitable economy. It was superior to heavy government control of early China, yet more self-correcting than the later Roman system of moral code and government. The ideal is always to have ethics rooted in individuals with government overseeing. It must be non intrusive, but profitable. Still it is highly sensitive to society and culture as a whole.

You might have said that all this overlooks the basic greed of individuals at the top. Greed is a serious problem; and as we have seen, greed erodes long-term profitability. It is here that government regulations are important. It is here that society's moral code and religious strengths also act as moderators. Still, history has shown that government and moral code are not the complete answer. The real answer is in individual leadership and personal commitment.

Maybe just as important in the issue of profitability and ethics is that ethical behavior is motivational. Ethical behavior assures the fair treatment of employees and that relates to bottom line profitability. Ethical behavior also assures economic balance. It is no accident in society that crime goes down as the economy goes up. If people can live well on an honest wage, many problems of society go away. This was at the heart of the early Roman success with ethics and profitability. The best way to motivate people is to treat them fairly.

Leadership – The Force Behind E-Profitability

One of the great scandals of the robber baron era occurred in 1890. It was centered on something similar to what we have discussed – falsification of steel testing records. The scandal centered on armor plate for the US Navy manufactured in Pittsburgh at Carnegie Steel. A number of low-level workers were the whistleblowers (with questionable motivations). Still after investigations, most agreed that record falsification had taken place. A long array of corporate officials was dragged to court. Some of these great leaders such as Charles Schwab testified they knew nothing about the falsification of records. After studying the historical record as well as my own more recent experience, I believe this was the truth. The top of the house really doesn't know and that is because they purposely choose not to know as well as organizational entropy. For example at many community colleges, presidents push the need for student retention. The professors are ready to please and can get over zealous viewing "retention" as passing students on. While these community college presidents didn't condone or ask for this, neither was it prohibited. The same is true in business. Ethics requires leadership and leadership is always proactive.

If we study the great steel scandals of the 1890s as well as the great business scandals of today, we find a lack of leadership at the top. We are also amazed to discover that the system is unethical and the upper managers are ignorant of the old behavior ingrained in the organization. We also find a short-term view, which in the end costs the company millions. Unethical behavior is entropic, which means that it ultimately must come to a disastrous end. Specifications will be stretched with the customer or field disaster causing a halt. Ethical people at the top don't even assure e-profitability. E-profitability requires proactive leadership at the top. You can't train, hire, or develop ethics in an organization; you can only instill ethics via leadership. Ultimately you create a culture to support it.

E-Profitability is Cultural

Ethical leadership is not paternal or managerial; it is cultural. The only role of top management is to create a culture that is ethical. An ethical culture is motivational by nature. Ethics is the best way to eliminate people and productivity problems. Ethics and profitability work together. However, it is not fair to put the ethical issues of business today solely on the business leadership. It goes to the national leadership and the concerns of American culture.

E-profitability requires a break in the mindset that ethics and profitability are not natural partners. This culture is a real American experience. The root of the successful Industrial Revolution was a strong religious and work ethic in the culture. Like ancient Israel, our religious foundation and political system acted as base. Political and business scandals occurred, but they did not define or create culture as we see today. Our society is more tolerant of unethical behavior—we rationalize and minimize it. Once in a case of student cheating, a professor suggested that we be tolerant of it because in their country of origin, cheating is culturally acceptable. This type of thinking brings us all down to the lowest level.

In fact, many sociologists of the last century such as Max Weber attributed America's success to its "Christian work ethic". Success depended on accountability to a higher power. Ethics and profitability went hand in hand, backed by a unified view of ethics in our culture.

This is not a lost concept. Many studies support the profitability of companies with high ethical standards. A forty-year study of companies from 1950 to 1990 with high ethical standards showed an 11.3 percent increase annually, which was double the Dow Jones average. This study was developed by James Burke (CEO of J&J) and included companies such as Xerox and Eastman Kodak.

Ethical Rules for High Productivity

1. Profitability can only improve by playing by the rules (requirements and specifications).

2. The top of the hierarchy is responsible for setting the tone of ethical behavior.

3. Absolute objectives must be given a priority to assure ethical lower-level decision-making is profitable long run.

4. Unethical adjustments to profitability reporting, long run assure unprofitability.

5. In a vacuum, middle and lower management will do whatever it takes to achieve what top management is perceived to want. Therefore, top management must clearly communicate what it wants and what is acceptable behavior to achieve it.

6. Unethical behavior is entropic; that is, it is a downward slow spiral once started.

7. Ethics is also cultural and environment-based. You can't manage or supervise ethical behavior; you must create an ethical culture.

"We demand that big business give people a square deal; in return we must insist that when anyone engaged in big business honestly endeavors to do right, he shall himself be given a square deal"-- Theodore Roosevelt

The entopic nature of ethics has a major impact on profitability as seen. The effect of ethics is much broader in organizations going to the heart of corporate infrastructure. In particular, ethical behavior directly affects individual productivity and therefore, profitability. Ethics must be part of corporate vision; you cannot supply ethics on a limited basis to organizational cells and departments. Ethics must be part of the infrastructure to be successful. It must be initiated and driven from the top. The core of success is in ethical behavior. Ethical behavior has a number of components, individual beliefs, peer behavior, society and top leadership. The executives have limited ability to offset the first two. The executive does control the most important factor that of leadership. Even in the most adverse environments, leadership can maintain ethical behavior throughout organizations. Ethical infrastructure is the responsibility and charge of top management, and it is uniquely the function of top management.

Before looking at developing infrastructure we need to develop the case for ethics and productivity. Many studies have shown this, but more research is needed in this area at the nation's business schools. One recent study done at the Harvard Business School showed a clear correlation between spirituality and profits in the workplace.[1] Another study by McKinsey & Co showed similar gains in productivity for ethical companies.[2] This study showed dramatically higher gains in operating earnings, return on investment, and stock prices. Ethical behavior may well be the most over looked tool for competitive advantage. History demonstrates a strong case that the most ethical organizations are the most productive. James Penny, founder of JCPenny, said, "Golden rule principles are just as necessary for operating a business profitably as are trucks, typewriters, twine". Similarly the Ritz-Carlton states, "take good care of your employees, and they will take good care of the guests." Ethical behavior is the only function that can assure consistency and fairness in organizations. Non-ethical behavior in the long run will result in costly reactions of the organizations to correct as well as a steady erosion of productivity. The union movement in the United States can directly be related to unethical corporate behavior. Unionization is an obvious and necessary reaction to unethical behavior but less visible is the daily loss of individual productivity due to unethical behavior. Hidden costs are the major issue in manufacturing with unethical behavior. They range from lower productivity to stealing and sabotage to full unionization.

Ethical behavior has moved beyond its ancillary role as a tool for competitive advantage. Ethics touches all phases of the business organization. The approach to ethics does vary from the proactive evangelical Christian approach of Chick-Fil-A to a more laid-back approach of Xerox. Ethics applied in Business crosses all religious boundaries. Jeffery

---

[1] Sept 2001
", Business Week, New York, November, 1999 Thomp, Executive Excellence, Provo,

Swartz of Shoemaker Timberland draws on his orthodox Jewish religious beliefs to make business decisions. For CEO Kris Kalra of BioGenex it's the Hindu text the Bhagavad-Gita, and for J.C. Penny, it was the Bible. The majority of these ethical based companies do stick to a cross-denominational, generic message.

The importance of ethics in corporate infrastructure revolves around employee and employer needs. In a 1994 study of business factors that affect where people want to work, the major factor was employee treatment followed by business practices. The postindustrial world has caused great anxiety in the workplace. Employees are under great pressure to conform or get out. Even worse is the practice of humiliation to punish employees. Employee abuse of law to take advantage of a company is a similar problem and may well have the same root cause.

Pay issues are also ethical issues. Fairness in pay is clearly the single most important issue in productivity. Malcolm Forbes put it straight forward – "Pay your people the least possible and you'll get from them the same". Forbes's view is the same as Henry Ford's when he instituted the $5 day in 1913. Ford was clearly no saint but was a pragmatic businessman. In actual fact prior to the $5 day Ford Motor was still one of the highest paying factories in the United States. Ford, however, was a wealthy company as well and the gap of the top and labor stood out to all. The discrepancy was part of the strong pressure being put on by the unionization movement. Ford's close friend Thomas Edison was an out spoken advocate of higher wages and profit sharing saying industry needed to "make this world over". When Ford Motor announced its combination of profit sharing to establish a $5 day it called "the greatest revolution in the matter of rewards for its workers ever known to the industrial world".

The relation of pay and ethics is understated in most business books and by most executives. It is not pay in absolute terms but the pay in individual perceptions of fairness. Employees can even accept a pay cut if the percept as necessary and fair. These issues are not always top corporate decisions, as many believe. Middle managers at times can control pay through overtime, assignments and training. Control of one's pay is a major trigger. Unfair practices or favoritism can cause reduction in productivity as employees adjust their "real" pay. This internal productivity cost can be extremely high. In one Midwestern (non-union) plant, pay in particular overtime was controlled by supervision via a "buddy" system. There was clearly an in and out group of employees. This buddy system evolved under an unethical management. Morale suffered as well as productivity. Fear worked in the short run to hold productivity but long run fear breaks sown in unethical workplaces. Vroom, in his expectancy theory showed that preceded lack of fairness in paying with cause a reaction to bring expectations into alignment with reality. Lack of ethics like oppression, will always stir a reaction in the hearts of men. These reactions maybe hidden but they will always be at work reducing productivity and profitability. Unchecked it will lead to some form of regulation such as unionization or government.

The Loss of Social Fabric

One result of the general erosion of ethics in society and the workplace is the lost of a true employer/employee social contract. The traditional social pact of the industrial era was an implied security-loyalty-paternalism pact. It supplied a social foundation through the workplace in the industrial paradigm. It was based on a Christian based morality of management. This stable unwritten agreement of management resulted in what has been called the "protestant work ethic" by employees. The traditional work social contract supplied an ethical foundation for corporations. This social foundation allowed for higher-level motivation techniques by managers for increased productivity. This family approach of companies supplied an ethical envelope for companies to work in. Productivity models in the industrial paradigm were based on a hierarchy of needs. Once very basic needs are meant, the employees tend to focus on the workplace environment. Ethical behavior was all but over looked in these early studies, yet without an ethical environment the realization of needs starts to breakdown. Without an ethical foundation issues like fair pay and treatment can lose meaning. Issues like ethics did start to be indirectly addressed by researchers in the 1960's.

One of the characteristics of our postindustrial era is the lack of a social work contract. One example of the industrial-post industrial transition is the experience of Weirton Steel in Weirton, West Virginia. Until the 1960's, Weirton Steel for decades had a "family" company. The city of Weirton and Weirton Steel functioned as integrated community. If you worked at Weirton Steel, your sons were assured a job. Many employees who were disabled in mill accidents were assigned to a lifetime of light duty. Widows and children of accidental deaths were helped financially. The company gave money to help community centers and churches. There was a loyalty and pride among the workers and the community. This family model was the heart of the ethical behavior that was Weirton Steel's hallmark. In the 60's, Weirton Steel was brought by steel conglomerate National Steel. Like so many of these postindustrial buyouts, it ended the family relationships of the original company. Of course the company line was the great steel recession required economic adjustments. The corporate policies and changes were dramatic. There was also a profound change in the hearts and minds of the employees. I was there in the seventies and the employee attitude was one of a mere economic exchange. Employees were no longer willing to sacrifice beyond that required. The love of the old company was still there but replaced with a new anger for National Steel.

Equity and Expectancy Theories

These theories accepted the fact that perceived unfair treatment would result in a productivity response by the individual. An employee who perceived himself or herself to be unfairly paid would adjust their output. This productivity response has been studied extensively in two-tier job structures. Here new hires are paid less for doing the same job as those with more time. Many companies like United Parcel Service, American Airlines, and most internationally unionized companies suffer from such pay structure that is perceived as inequitable. This doesn't mean that such systems are unethical but the perception is at least unfair. The situation becomes much more problematic when the case is unethical, such as the case where overtime is given on a favoritism basis.

Negative perception is a powerful anti-motivator when unethical behavior is involved. The reaction can cause ethical erosion throughout the organization. Drops in productivity and things like employee pillage in the infrastructure result of unethical management practices. Studies have clearly demonstrated that the organization and individuals will adjust for inequitable and unethical conditions. No company can expect a "work ethic" in employees unless there is an organizational ethic. Unethical behavior by middle and lower management is one of the great unaccounted for productivity losses.

Some Historical Roots

China was one of the earliest industrial countries to address ethics and productivity. In an historical document known as *The Record of Etiquette* (300BC), business ethics is clearly addressed. The idea of fair pay for a fair days work is addressed widely in the Bible.

Managers today complain often of the restrictive and costly demands of unions. Unfortunately we are paying for the sins of fathers and grandfathers. Unions are the product of the equity and expectancy theories in unethical companies. Unfair and unethical behavior always results in a response in the organizations. Companies that over the years have consistently demonstrated ethical behavior have been resistant to unionization. Japanese transplant and joint venture operations in this country have built strong ethical bases resulting in a perception of fairness. This has resulted in failures of the international autoworkers to unionize these plants. Ethical and fair behavior is clearly the substitute for a union. I'm not antiunion; they play an important role but bring their own ethical issues to the table. Regardless of union and non-union employees ethical behavior is always a plus to productivity.

Ethical behavior by its very nature is fair. Fairness and perception are central to individual and corporate productivity. Many management scientists over the years have noted the relationship of ethical management and productivity. In 1923, British management expert, Oliver Sheldon suggested a management creed. Sheldon was one of the earliest to pen the premise that ethical management is a prequisite for employee loyalty and productivity. He further suggested the need to train managers in ethics for the purpose of increased productivity. Sheldon realized that ethics was a basis of motivation –"An effort should be made toward the promotion of individual and corporate effectiveness of effort through leadership and equitable discipline". Sheldon based this premise on Henri Fayol basic 14 points of management (Fayol is known as the "Francis Bacon" of management literature). One of Fayol's points was equity of treatment. Fayol stated: "For the personnel to be encouraged to carry out its duties with all the devotion and loyalty of which it is capable it must be treated with kindliness, and equity results from the combination of kindliness and justice". Fayol had a strong belief that organizations and individuals in them have a basic desire for equity and equality. Equity while originating at the top must be applied consistently throughout the whole organization. This requires a strong mission statement and policy. Organization training is also a requirement, if equity is to foster in an organization.

In the beginning of the 1800's an ethical light shown through the dark smoke of industrial Scotland. It was the textile mills of Robert Owen in New Lanark. Owens was the first to demonstrate that ethical management is profitable. Owens's mills were revolutionary in their approach to a paternalistic treatment to employees. This was in stark contrast to his competitors of the time, which supplied Charles Dickens so much material. Industrial England believed cheap labor to be the engine of industrialization. Owens made a bold prediction to fellow owners-"Your living machines may be easily trained and directed to procure a large increase of pecuniary gain. Money spent on employees might give a 50 to 100 per cent return as opposed to a 15 per cent return on machinery. The economy of living machinery is to keep it neat and clean, treat it with kindness that its mental movements might not experience too much irritating friction."

The most outspoken early writer was Max Weber from 1910 to 1930. While a great deal of Weber's work has been proven, a lot has been refuted. Weber thesis was very limited and self serving but did touch on the underlying importance of ethics to profitability. We will see later that what Weber attributed to the "protestant work ethic" can be equally applied to all of the great religions.

Conclusions and Actions

1. Ethical behavior is a foundation for individual and corporate productivity. Ethical management assures that equity is fostered throughout the organization.

2. A fully integrated ethical infrastructure is required. Middle and front line management need to part of their ethical approach on productivity breakdowns.

3. Corporate ethics is a two-way interaction. Work ethics is the product of corporate ethical behavior.

4. Ethical behavior does not fit the traditional extension of theory as a dis-satisfier (hygiene factor). Ethical behavior in our new view is a basic motivation.

5. Individual beliefs, peer pressure, society, corporate culture and leadership affect ethical behavior.

Principles of Business Ethics

Ethics are approached in various ways in business. Textbooks tend to categorize these principles in terms like categorical imperative disclosure rule, utilitarian principal, etc. In practice I find that there are three basic approaches- the Golden Rule, intuition and utilitarian. The Golden Rule is straight forward "Do unto others as you would have them do unto you". Intuition is that gut feel of right and wrong. Production tend to take shortcuts to "save money" or time which is also reflected in ethics that crosses all religions. For example Confucius stated a rule of life as: "what you do not want done to yourself, do not do to others". The Confucian principle is the negative statement of the Golden Rule! A Hindu guide states: "Men gifted with intelligence and purified souls should always treat others as they wish to be treated." The great Robbi Hillel stated: "What thou thyself hatest, do not do to thy neighbor. That is the whole law. The rest is commentary. Go and learn it." Clearly there is board religious support for what Martin Luther called the "natural law" of the Golden Rule. The Golden Rule's universality and simplicity are probably the real secret of its popularity.

While survey after survey supports the Golden Rule as the number one standard of ethics in business, actual application of the rule is not as clear. Like Christianity and other religions application often falls far short of the ideals. This again is the responsibility of leadership. The Golden Rule must be part of corporate vision as well as mission. Too many times the use of the Golden Rule is defensive rather than a proactive productivity tool.

The power of the Golden Rule is that it is a motivational tool. The Golden Rule fully applied can eliminate employee problems and negativity. The rule can supply the fairness that is the universal quest of employees in general. It goes a long way in assuring good supervision. The other strength of the rule is it is universal acceptance regardless of religious or lack of religious beliefs.

Its weakness is in the lack of leadership and resolve that accompanies its use. It is better to have the Golden Rule in the belief system versus the mission statement. This requires a commitment and a belief that the golden rule will make for a better and more profitable workplace. If we look at Max Weber's great tribute to the Golden Rule's rule in the Industrial Revolution, we still see that application fell far short of the ideals. Society's belief was, however, stronger in that time period.

Academia's talk of a complementary rule of the Golden Rule is known as the "Disclosure Rule" The "Disclosure Rule" asks that you make decisions based on whether you are comfortable if all your associates, friends, and family were aware of your decisions. This view has popularity approaching that of the Golden Rule. However in practice it lacks the clarity and moral authority of the Golden Rule. That makes it even more difficult to apply. While considered an inferior technique in most research surveys, in practice it is the most widely used. It is an extremely subjective approach that holds to no moral or ethical standard. As the ethical and moral codes of society disappear, intuition becomes even more dangerous in application. Intuition makes gods out of managers and perspective is lost. Intuition can be used to justify anything. Intuition is a very poor approach to ethical practices. It actually increases corporate entropy and disorder.

Utilitarian Approach

The utilitarian approach aims at the greater good for the greater number. The great English philosopher Jeremy Benthon (1748-1832) said, "The greatest happiness of the greatest number is the foundation of morals and legislation". It is not a weak approach if you are god and many executives believe they are. It becomes easy to layoff a 100 employees to save the jobs of 1000 employees. However it can be very short sided because intuition is used in practice. For example, a pay cut could have saved all the 100 jobs. The fundamental principle of utilitarianism was proposed by two nineteenth century philosophers- Jeremy Benthon and John Stuart Mill. It was an effort to help one-make decisions in light of the greater good. From an historical perspective Benthon and Mill were dealing with very different society and cultural base. Society to a large degree supplied the moral background and minimum ethical standards. We cannot count on society today. The utilitarian approach has no standard or core values to formulate decisions.

It's even worse than not having help from a moral society, its actually the negative impact of society. The core values become those of a segment of society. It's a society where presidents can twist words and views. It's a definitional justification or legalistic ethics that our society allows. It's using dope but not inhaling or confusing intent with definitions. President Clinton re-defined sex or maybe as he viewed it, he actually defined it. This definitional or legalistic approach to ethics is defensive in nature. Yet it can be used to justify one's approach. Utilitarian principle has been evolved often to justify one plant closing over another.

The models we have discussed so far are more theoretical than pragmatic. Corporate integrity is an approach pioneered by IBM. Modern philosopher Mark Halfin defines integrity as "a consistent commitment to do what is best- especially under conditions of adversity." Still what does "best" mean? It is here that IBM applies its Kantian version of the Golden Rule. Immanuel Kant, an 18th century philosopher, defined moral code as, "no person's rights should be subordinated to anyone else". The IBM core value is "Respect for the individual." IBM's approach realizes that a frog making a decision to jump off the log is not the same as a frog actually jumping off the log. It is here that IBM uses culture to reinforce individual integrity.

IBM's contribution to business ethics is its use of culture to make integrity work. This is done via rules, employee codes, and corporate training. The real success, however, is tied to leadership. In the early 1990's, John Ahers, chairman of IBM, stated, "IBM has always understood that integrity has helped the organization build strategic advantage." This is the real essence of ethics; ethical behavior and fairness will increase profitability. When leaders make this connection the end result will be strategic advantage. Furthermore it leads to commitment in the workplace. Finally IBM is not alone in seeing the link between profitability and ethics of companies like Herman Miller and J.C. Penny are working hard to make the link.

Ethical behavior is always a reflection of corporate culture; and culture, of course, permeates the organization. Cheating on expensive accounts can be expected throughout an organization like Enron, which had corrupt top management. Corruption is cultural in many cases. Sure there are individual cases of corruption possible in some companies but without a supporting culture it is short lined. There is an interaction of applied ethics and corporate culture that causes an evolution of a unique approach for organizations. College textbooks of business ethics overlooked these key relationships. Models are used instead, but culture is the foundation of business ethics.

One difference I noticed in my career at various companies showed this relationship. One company was very aggressive about copyright laws in the early days of personal computers. Copying of software was banned by written policy. The company asked middle managers to buy software not to illegally copy it. This was a society where copying software was viewed as "ok". Such a policy was "costly" but it sent a message of dedication to ethical behavior. The positive is that software costs were more than offset by more ethical behavior by employees on expense accounts, supplier etc. This is an example of ethical leadership and culture building. It may surprise you that this was again LTV steel, which I discussed earlier on un-ethical behavior. These paradoxes are to be expected because culture sets moral standards of what's acceptable. It shows that leadership, while maybe the most important, is not the only input into corporate culture. Ethical principles such as the Golden Rule must be embedded in mission statement and written policy. Ethics must be part of training as well. Society has an impact as well. Society's ethical views have been lowered over the years. This puts more of the burden on corporate leadership. Many see the decline of morals in society as the real issue. Others agree that the economy is the real problem. An early prophet of industrial ethics (Bishop Sheen) said, "It is not the economy that is the problem, but a lack of the spirit."

1. Mission/Vision is the DNA of ethics leadership

It is at the very heart of any corporation approach to ethics. Approaches vary from mission, vision, and policy statements. Companies with strong ethics programs such as Johnson and Johnson, GTE and Hewlett-Packard embedded ethics in the mission statement and have separate credos as well. A reference to ethics is created in the mission statement. Of course most mission statements are a poor substitute for art hanging on the walls. We are conditioned by standards such as ISO 9000 to use couplets of buzzwords such as customer satisfaction and continuous improvement. However ethics in a mission statement stands out and ethics must start in the mission statement. The mission statement is the keystone to the building of an ethical foundation.

After the mission statement, policy statements must reinforce culture development. Many companies such as Boeing, Norton, GTE, and Chemical Bank publish guidelines. These are needed for leadership to work effectively. Executives, like all employees, come and go, so that policy and mission need to put ethics up front and establish a time resistant corporate memorial to a culture of ethics. Culture must be in place to strengthen and focus top leadership. Culture outlasts management change and therefore is a necessity base.

Culture building must also include ethical infrastructure, which includes management structure and training. Training is another must. Training is an instrument of culture building. Things like ethics committees, ombudsmen, and employee hot lines can be regulatory but are not necessary culture buildings. Management infrastructure would focus on training as culture building more so than regulatory infrastructure. Disney is well known for its employee course known as Disney 101. A similar course is needed in all companies particularly on the company's ethical view. It is in these first employee interactions that culture is built and reinforced. Universities with a record of high alumni giving have one thing in common; they start alumni giving programs with their freshman orientations. It is in these orientations that the traditions are passed to the freshman. Pride and loyalty are developed at orientation that carries a lifetime.

2. Leadership

Culture must be considered a prerequisite to leadership. Without a cultural framework leadership cannot arise or sustain. Given this leadership is the backbone of ethical behavior. Leadership must be spearheaded throughout the management levels. Any significant gap in ethical behavior between management levels results in a corporate wide break down. Still the focus must start at the top where policy originates. Policy, standards and mission integration are tasks of corporate leadership. Middle managers need to step up to the plate as examples. Many times employees look first to their direct supervisors as to how policy will apply. Leadership requires obedience and proactive support to make policy work.

Ethical leadership requires a few specific notes. Ethical leadership is always leadership by example. In fact managers must take the forefront with ethics. Often leadership and ethics require stands against the "acceptable norm". It requires strict adherence to policy but that is only a minimum. Proactive leadership is needed such as verbal support of the policy in even causal conversations. There can be no debate, ethical leadership demands obedience throughout management. With ethics, managers at all levels live in a glass office. That is also why culture and leadership need to work in tandem.

Leadership not only sets a daily example but also rises to meet defining corporate moments. The University of Michigan has a very proud tradition of academics and sports. In the 1980's Michigan basketball recruited a dream team of freshman players known as the "Fab Five". The national publicity was enormous and sports promoters and gamblers were drawn to the story. With the teams success came a nightmare of discipline problems for the coach. In addition professional gamblers and sports promoters grew ever close to players. The result was unethical and illegal activities by the players. The players' success held the coach, alumni and administration hostage. The university failed to manage the problem but that was not the driving force. The scandal broke years later and continued for the university and the players for years into the next century. The proof of the player's role in point shaving and other illegal activities became clear as time passed. The new president of the university in 2002 took a leadership role. She did not wait for further NCAA review and decisions but applied internal penalties. This included surrendering a National Championship and all references to it. A year suspension on the present team plus a number of smaller restrictions was also imposed. By not waiting for the NCAA, the university gave a strong message to the whole university community about ethical behavior. The president sent the strongest message possible and it has had an enduring effect. The university could have waited and took a defensive role with some justification, and escaped with minor penalties. Waiting, however, would have not set the tone of the need to apply ethical behavior. When there is questioning in an organization, leadership must come forward.

Profitability and the Global View of Ethics

Ethical behavior impacts profitability beyond the internal infrastructure. Ethical behavior can dramatically increase profits via customer, supplier, and community relationships. In particular, cooperative networks are developed that impacts the profitability and productivity of the overall network. Ethics in particular can have huge payback in this area. While most textbooks on ethics talk of "stakeholders", I prefer to use traditional identification of these business relationships.

Customer Relationships

I spent many years in quality control trying to solve customer problems. Many times small problems became large problems because we were not upfront early on with the customer. Let me share an actual example of a problem with LTV and General Motors. LTV's bar division supplied steel in the 1980's for General Motors to forge and manufacture axles and front wheel spindles. These front wheel spindles hold the cars wheels on. The steel required needed to be free of "dirt" embedded in the steel body. Embedded dirt can cause the spindle to break under load. Control of embedded dirt is a major and expensive production process. Production tends to take shortcuts to "save money" or time which is also reflected in dollars. In the case of several batches of steel, production management had tried some new faster techniques without involving quality control or the necessary technical people. This production-quality control gamesmanship is a result of a lack of a strong ethical culture discussed in earlier chapters.

In this case like so many, the change surfaced as a customer crisis. In this case a front wheel spindle broke and a wheel fell off a GMC Vice President's car! Samples to the LTV lab showed the dirt embedded and the root analysis started. Quality control identified the batch and in the investigation uncovered the production change. Since the batch, which the spindle came from, was already several months old it suggested that a great of steel was already in General Motors cars. Notifying General Motors of the nature and extent of the problem might result in a recall and millions of dollars in cost to LTV. The decision was made to present (assure) the problem to General Motors as a one batch problem.

General Motors was suspicious since it was known that LTV and Republic Steel rarely were upfront with them. General Motors started testing all the steel on hand and found more dirt. It was then clear to General Motors this was a larger problem than they have been told. While working on the problem ourselves, we did not tell General Motors of the process change. This was clearly a mistake and certainly questionable ethics. Fear took over that froze common sense even because of the possibility of a company breaking automotive recall. The crisis grew as we stonewalled General Motors. As usual quality control forces every one to come clean because of overwhelming personal pressure and stress. Once everything was on the table, both parties worked to resolve the problem and make good joint decisions on how to best resolve the problem. Working together we could identify and trace possible problem batches of steel at General Motors and LTV. If this had been done on day one of the problem it would have never evolved in a possible recall crisis. Furthermore had operations management been up front and the proper testing been done to assure the process change would not cause a dirt problem. This is example of how poor ethical behavior is a source of operating costs. The cost of this operating process change eventually was over a million dollars. An upfront cooperative effort internally at a minor cost could have avoided this.

Stories like that of General Motors and LTV are common in American industry. These stories are not necessarily bad people doing bad things, but a lack of corporate infrastructure to assure that the right things are done. If we look at the Firestone-Ford tire scandal of recent years we see the same story. Such stories cause an outcry of the lack of ethics and corruption in American industry. The real issues are much more subtle and basic to all humans. Fear is at the heart of these quality problems. First the fear of the worker to report mistakes to a supervisor who might punish harshly. Fear of the middle manager to impact the plant's profitability and potentially viability creates a cover up. Fear of top management to lose a customer that may cause a corporate bankruptcy causes more cover up. Fear is as natural in the world as entropy. Corporate ethics is the infrastructure needed to manage fear in organizations as well as the supplier-customer extension. Edward Deming, the famous quality guru, had fourteen points for successful management. One of those points was "eliminate fear". Take fear away at the lowest level in an organization and scandals like that of Firestone of the last decade disappear.

Fear needs to be broken in customer/supplier relationships and that leads to another one of Deming's fourteen points-"reduce the number of suppliers". The reason for this reduction was to build closer customer relationships. When there are as there are typically in American industry many suppliers, problems are resolved by throwing out a supplier. This dramatic loss causes more fear because so much is on the line. Deming believed in long term relationships, which required working through problems with a supplier. In the long run the practice of using and playing suppliers against each other to gain improvements actually increases costs. Customer/supplier openness can become a core of long term profitability by working honestly through the problem. Even in its later stages of the Firestone scandal, the problem could have been resolved cheaply if there had been openness and trust on the part of Ford and Firestone. Trust and openness are the heart of ethical management.

The discussion prior shows the typical relationship approach in manufacturing. It's an adversarial relationship that lacks trust and honesty for sure. What are often overlooked are the day-to-day costs of this type of operation. This is particularly true of business-to-business relationships, which do not come under government regulations that you see in the business to consumer relationships. Poor ethical relationships are the true hidden costs of the business-to-business relationships. It is an area that cannot be addressed easily by regulations or rules.

Of course, the same holds true in retailing. There was a midwestern gasoline station that had a poorly calibrated pump. It registered about three times the amount of gas pumped. To most customers the time and speed of the meter signaled something was wrong. The owner refused to listen to the customer complaints or worse saw an "opportunity" to take profits. The problem went on for a week or more. Short run the owner benefited but the long run effects were deep. Customers burnt once refused to return. Some of these had been local long-term customers. Within a few months the owner went out of business as volume dropped off. Even the new owner suffers from the poor ethics of the previous owner.

Supplier Relationships

There's an old business adage that says you make your profit when you buy not when you sell. Supplier relationships are part of the business network affected by ethical behavior. Costs are driven up for every one with poor or unethical supplier relationships. Supply chain ethics has always been a hot spot for corporate ethical problems. It is an area that requires written policies and reasonable policies. Suppliers generally do business via lunches, parties, gifts and sporting events. These activities are extensive throughout management structure. They are not necessarily unethical but they must be covered via policy. In the late eighties when Chrysler imposed across the board price cuts to its suppliers, suppliers pointed to the high "costs of doing business". Unfortunately policy statements and proactive leadership are required in this area since our natural tendencies and business methods cannot be trusted. Again many times the real hidden costs of unethical behavior occurs much below the headline executive stars. LTV tried to follow Chrysler in price cuts and had similar supplier out cries. Acceptable gifts were held to $25 and prior to dinners and sporting events written approval from division management was required. At the time I was in quality control and operations, which accepted these as reasonable (it was a pain from our previous freedom). Within a few months the policy was ignored because the Vice President of Purchasing did not fully buy in.

It is an area that the Japanese claim greater success at reducing costs. The Japanese with strong national identity apply a national version of the utilitarian approach-that is the greater good for the greater number. The Japanese look at the whole supply chain to distribute costs for the overall good. For example in the United States quality improvement is an imposed unilateral effort. The customer in the supply chain uses it position to force product improvements on the supplier. This is common in automotive and heavy manufacturing. Quality improvements, however motivated, might seem like a good ideal. It can be extremely costly overall to the end customer or consumer.

A typical example can illustrate this with General Motors supply chains. It is a common approach for General Motors to demand, pod, and cajole for tighter standards and tolerances of raw materials and parts. Lets consider a ball bearing made to a plus or minus five ten thousands of the diameter. A ball bearing made to a tighter tolerance would reflect tighter process control and quality. The real issue is many times GM cannot realize any cost improvement or quality in the use of the ball bearing in the automotive subassembly. The tighter processing comes at an increased cost to the ball bearing maker, which must be passed on (or with GMC eaten) with no overall cost reduction to the chain. The reason for this lack of commitment to the overall good and trust is a product of historical unethical corporate behavior. This type of adversarial relationship costs not only higher prices but also many times plant closing. This leads us to the ideal of social responsibility as part of corporate ethics.

Social Responsibility

Kaoru Ishikawa, the Japanese father of quality, in his book "What is Total Quality Control" attributed the high of products in Japan to the basic philosophy of Mencius Confucianism as well as Buddhism. Ishikawa whose experience goes back to pre war Japan sees its strength in the ethics of its faith. Amazingly his writing resembles the claim of Max Weber as to the role of Christianity in America's success. In particular Ishikawa sees the use of the famed Japanese quality circles as "humanity in the workplace". Ishikawa like Weber to fit their beliefs to the success. Both Weber and Ishikawa wrote about national economies at the peak of their strength. They did, however, touch on the important role of ethics in revolutionizing the workplace. The problem with applying either Weber's or Ishikawa's theory is that neither deal well with the diversity of many workplaces. They both saw things in only one religious view. Both attacked other religious backgrounds as inferior. For example Ishikawa saw Christianity as lacking the humanity of Eastern religions. Weber attacked fellow Christians such as Catholics. Ethics require the support of the great religions but ethical behavior must be universal in nature.

Social responsibility is the natural out growth of ethical management. While it is part of all mainstream religions, it dos not require any particular religious view to be socially responsible.

Community

Community, the workplace, and ethics form an integrated system of responsibility. This relationship has been the most strained in the last fifty years. For many thousands of years community and the workplace were physically close and interrelated. I have lived through the great shift of this industrial system to that of a postindustrial era. Going back much earlier to the change of society from an agricultural one to an industrial mix. Towns and cities tended to be self sufficient as communities. There was an ethical responsibility to the communities where industry bloomed. Many industrialists were well aware of this link to the community. We have already discussed the success of Robert Owens's New Lanark but there were many more. Owen built recreation centers and schools for his community.

Oliver Sheldon had written extensively on the bond a manufacturer should have with the community in his *Philosophy of Management* (1923). Sheldon, like Owens, believed that developing the social and communal links of the worker was analogous to preventive maintenance on machines. The ideas of Sheldon stood in stark comparison to the view of industrial England as seen by Charles Dickens. Sheldon in particular fused social ethics with that of scientific management. Sheldon's success at the coca works of Rowntree & Company and Owen's success at New Lanark did have a profound effect on many industrialists. Tough business men like Westinghouse, Ford, Carnegie, Firestone and many others took note and tried to incorporate social ethics in their businesses.

Carnegie built libraries in the towns where he had mills. The link was many times criticized as pure business versus social ethics but he preserved. One of Carnegie's most beautiful libraries was given to the steel town of Homestead after the bitter strike of 1892. The Homestead strike was a bloody one with several deaths, which left his image tarnished. Carnegie did, however, have a strong community view. While the donated libraries stand today as architectural masterpieces, he supplied no books. Carnegie believed the relationship of business and community needed to be forged in mutual commitment. The responsibility for the books was with the community. These libraries are still today improving generations of Americans. I personally owe my love of writing and education to my boyhood love affair with the Carnegie Library of Oakland. He truly believed it was better to teach a person to plant than to supply food. Even his heirs were given only enough of the inheritance to live out their lives so the future generations would not be corrupted or un- motivated by excess money. Work was central to Carnegie's view of society. Carnegie inspired a number of his managers to do similar things. Charles Schwab (first president of US Steel and Bethlehem Steel) gave churches to worker communities.

George Westinghouse arrived at the same place from a different starting place. Carnegie's view fits what we had discussed as Utilitarian. George Westinghouse was a believer in the Golden Rule. Westinghouse built Christian community centers for his workers besides being one of the first to institute a pension plan. Furthermore Westinghouse supported local technical schools to educate his workers and families. Westinghouse was known also to avoid layoffs that would devastate communities. In his approach Westinghouse demonstrated the superiority of a Golden Rule over the utilitarian or disclosure approach.

Today we see many companies giving to the community. In many cases these are substantial donations. Still in economic crisis these same companies inflect massive layoffs on the community. Westinghouse, using the moral backing of the Golden Rule, actually achieved a better end result with the community. For example the early practice of giving turkeys to employees was terminated to start the funding of a pension program! There's a theory common in our postindustrial era that maybe called the good of the survivor rule. The idea is not to cut salaries, parties, turkeys etc but layoff and maintain these perks for the survivors. Many managers believe this eliminates the morale problems. The fat survivor policy merely hides the morale problem.

Chapter Ten

Business in a Global Economy

Cooperative Advantage versus Competitive Advantage

The issue concerns profits and productivity, not the method or philosophy. The great industrial empires of the past teamed up with customers, suppliers, competitors, unions, and government. Competition to the death is a mistake in a global market. Today our companies are competing with international trusts and combinations, yet our laws reflect the robber baron logic of the past. We need to look once again at the controlled efficiencies of Morgan, Carnegie, and Libbey's use of vertical and hortizontal trusts. The measure was success, not market dominance. The future belongs to the most cooperative, not the fittest.

Capital and labor are pitted against each other, losing the political power needed for job creating policy. Compromise is also difficult in such an adversarial environment, but that is what is needed. The same can be said for suppliers and customers. Suppliers are often given ultimatums on price and quality.

Innovation

The major source of competitive advantage is innovation. Innovation trumps cheap labor, low taxes, and raw materials. Over and over, these icons used innovation to build their companies. They battled in global markets equal to those of today. Many times the only advantage was technology. The source of innovation was always the full employee base, not a lone inventor. Innovation is a corporate function as shown by the business icons. Furthermore, innovation should be integrated into the corporate structure, not be a separate function or department.

Edison, Westinghouse, Michael Owens, and Charles Schwab differed a great deal in the methodology of innovation, but did have points of agreement. All set specific metric and time goals. Top management took responsibility for project selection and monitoring progress. All had a passion for innovation, and demanded that of those involved. Goals and passion seemed to trump any particular methodology.

Middle Management

Middle management is the keystone of the corporate and business infrastructure. Middle managers take the corporate vision and merge it with the employees' personal needs to maximize productivity. Middle managers supply the flexibility to blend strategic plans with tactical adjustments. They are the motivators of the organization. Middle Management today suffers from its Ozzie Nelson image of the 1950s, and has become a target of downsizing. Middle management needs to be strengthened, not eliminated.

The icons seemed consistent on the need for middle management, but not just the positions. A motivated middle management corps was key to people, like Schwab, Libbey, Jones, McKinley, Westinghouse, and even Ford. Middle managers convert the dreams of leadership into reality. The great icons saw middle managers as profit centers, not cost centers.

Top Management

Top management defines the vision and creates culture. It defines the culture by example. Real systems depend on top management's support, not supervision. Top management must, in some form, include the worker in the decision making process to develop trust. Rigorous honesty must be the hallmark of sharing financial information.

Top management must led and direct innovation, process improvement, and even invention. Project selection is part of that responsibility. Six-sigma, SPC, Kazien, and other improvement programs are "self-directed," lacking impact and breakthrough potential.

Shared Responsibility of Labor and Capital

We need to share the problems of employee benefits in a world of global competition. The government must also be part of the solution. Employees must take on the responsibility for their future with the company and government. Carnegie gave libraries, expecting the community to supply the books; Dickson expected employees to match company contributions to the pension plan; and McKinley demanded equal control of wages and tariffs. Ownership of capital in some form, such as profit sharing, needs to be explored. More importantly, labor and capital need a political alliance as seen during the McKinley administration. It was an alliance that included Gompers and Morgan for the shared goal of more business for America.

Culture

Culture, not infrastructure, defines an organization. Culture must be created and maintained. Vision is the DNA of culture. It was the hallmark of all the iconic leaders interviewed. Mentors, training, and leadership must vitalize culture. Culture must support corporate mission and vision.

A Belief in Capitalism and Self-Reliance

With all the inherent problems and propensity to greed, these icons believed in capitalism. Often they abused their power, but at times they demonstrated an understanding dirived from their lower class roots. They loved to recall their social climb and rags-to-riches stories. A few, like Dickson, Owen, McKinley, Jones, Owens, and Gompers believed in the totally fair treatment and equality of the worker. They had a vision of an industrial democracy. They believed in the supremacy of the United States, and valued manufacturing as America's core. Exceptionalism was the term applied by most that is a belief in the leadership of American principles.

American exceptionalism was both a concept and a responsibility. If tariffs generated profits than investment was to be expected. Labor was almost expected to participate in the financial growth of companies. Government's role was to assure all lived up to their responsibilities.

Ownership

Ownership was another common theme in this iconic era. These leaders often struggles on how to achieve that ownership, but they believed in its need. The methods varied form Robert Owen's communal approach to Carnegie's stock plans to the ancillary support of Westinghouse. The point remained that employee need to feel some part of the operation. Samuel Gompers viewed the union as a means of sharing capital. They realized that security was a necessity, but there were other needs too. Their behavior reflected a built-in understanding of what would later be defined as

Maslow's hierarchy of needs. Most realized that ownership was at the heart of capitalism, and needed to refute the rise of socialism.

Maybe just as important is that these icons realized ownership is more than owning a few stock shares. Ownership means having a say in decisions. There must be a sharing of gains and sacrifices as well.

Goals and Rewards

This stands out with these leaders. They set and focused on goals. They preferred bonuses on achieving goals as a motivator. They worshiped achievement over money. They preferred management by objectives, focusing on individual motivation, versus general wage or profit-sharing increases. They hired only achievement-oriented employees, building a culture of achievement in their organizations. These bonuses made many financially secure, if not wealthy, in all classes.

Supply Chains Compete, Not Companies

This was another view of these icons. It drove them to horizontal integration, which generated economies of scale. Today, supply chain networks can be built while retaining separate companies, but a new type of supply chain management is needed. It may be that supply chain logistics companies need a new paradigm of separate but shared management. Someone needs to manage the overall good of the supply chain versus top feeding of the chain's resources.

Design can be a Competitive Advantage

Product design is like innovation. It needs to be improved and honed to gain advantage. America has let this one-time strength decline since the 1950s. Furthermore, design must be integrated through suppliers, manufacturing, and the customer. Design is a human skill enhanced product attribute and needs to be exploited.

Diagnostic Inspection versus Sort

Inspection should sort and help one find the root cause in the process. While they believe inspection should be a separate function, the inspector should be selected from the process operators. Operating experience allows the inspector to search for root causes in the process. Inspector/operator rotation offers the ideal mix to man inspection units.

Globalization is Inevitable

Accept it as a way of life and use it to your advantage. The way to prosper with globalization is innovation, technology, design, and cooperative advantage. Leverage the characteristics of globalization such as free trade, cheap labor, outsourcing, and the Internet. The winners of globalization are logistics companies, shipping companies, Internet companies, cheap labor, temporary labor, telecommunications, robots, modular manufacturers, innovators, evolving countries, and free traders. The losers of globalization are middlemen, unions, high price labor, car dealers, neo-Luddites, specialized trades, and industrialized countries. Globalization requires a cooperative effort of business, unions, communities, workers, managers, and government.

Competing in global markets will require a new paradigm for all. Bigness is not the enemy, but a necessity. Business, labor, and government must set national goals and cooperate for success. Policies need to be developed on what is needed for American business. Unions and capital must come to accept a unified vision, mission, and strategy.

Robotics are the key to the Future

The iconic managers of the past were committed to technology and automation. Robots are the next source of cheap, efficient labor. They are reliable and consistent, addressing the major cost in manufacturing- absenteeism. The country that takes leadership will dominate the future. Companies need to aggressively apply robotics and automation. Long run automation creates jobs through market growth. Unfortunately, the United States lags behind Japan in robot development and manufacture. We need to sponsor competition, and divert tax dollars into research grants.

The Best Guide is the Golden Rule

That is, you treat people, as you want to be treated. It's a simple principle exhibited by all the icons. The corollary is that people make the profits that pay the bills. This theme can be considered an iconic law. These icons had their share of problems, but they tried to be fair. At times, their philosophies seemed harsh, but they tried to the best of their ability to balance the needs of the worker and business.

Carnegie and Schwab made plenty of mistakes, but they tried to adjust for them. We are human and we can expect mistakes, wrong turns, and even greed, but trying is important. People like Westinghouse, Owen, Follett, and Jones had better battling averages. They proved that playing by the rules could result in profits.

Government's Role is to Develop, Foster, and Manage an Environment for a Strong Job Creating American Economy

The present strategy lacks a vision and a mission for our nation. The government should set goals for business projects requiring large amounts of and coordinated resources, such as the gasoline free car. Furthermore, the government should be proactive in education and training, instead of passive retraining of displaced workers. Government needs to supply technology leadership and development. Scholarships, grants, loans, national industrial fairs, competitive awards, and elementary education should be used to foster a national passion for technology, engineering, and science. Businesses and local communities need to pool resources for competitive advantage.

The tariff-trade debate needs to be raised. The consumer benefits from the "free" trade approach of today, but at what cost? In many cases, we are paying for these lower prices with our health benefits, pensions, and wages. McKinley's *reciprocity* needs a new look. We need to consider, as Adam Smith suggests, a core industry. Government needs to monitor and react to abuses both nationally and internationally. Jobs should never be sacrificed or traded for international political goals.

Quality is Not First or Free, but One of Several Goals

Quality must be integrated with cost, delivery, deign, and ease of manufacture. Quality is not free and should command a fair price from customers. If quality is critical then one should pay for it. Fredrick Taylor demonstrated that pushing quality first (or production first) results in internal problems. Quality, production, and safety must be integrated.

Supply chains should compromise for the overall good of the chain on the level of quality needed for the end product. ISO 9000 properly applied supplies the necessary balance.

A Business and Labor Alliance

This was a foundation of the iconic period. The alliance crossed political lines for the good of all. It stands in stark contrast to today. J. P. Morgan and Samuel Gompers agreeing to expand business trusts seems strange today, but the jobs were the real agreement between the two. They came together to promote mutual goals. There were problems, but the alliance helped shape a policy for jobs. Right now policy on trade is decided on the greater good for the consumer, which is the biggest political element. Consumers do follow Adam Smith principles of self-survival, and their diversity makes them apolitical as a group. A business/labor alliance could change things and balance our trade approach. Business and labor need to cooperate to gain political advantage. This alliance should shape policy, not be shaped by it. Such an alliance would have to be respected by both political parties. With the exception of Adam Smith and possibly Carnegie, it is a central lesson of the interviews.

Appendix

Process Capability

Cp called "inherent capability" or "potential capability"

$$Cp = \frac{\text{Specification width or range}}{\text{Process width or six sigma}}$$

$$Cp = \frac{\text{Upper spec limit- lower spec limit}}{6 \text{ sigma}}$$

Cpk called actual capability or whether the process is centered

Cpk = the minimum of

$$\frac{\text{Lower spec} - \text{process average}}{3 \text{ sigma}}$$

Or

$$\frac{\text{Process average- Lower spec}}{3 \text{ sigma}}$$

Cp and Cpk should be greater than one for theoretical process capability. TS 16949 require 1.66 as a safety factor. 1.33 is generally considered a good safety factor.